DR. FURTADO was formerly Chief of the Development Division of CEPAL (Economic Commission for Latin America), Director of the Banco Nacional do Desenvolvimento Económica in Rio de Janeiro, Executive Head of the Agency for the Development of the Brazilian Northeast, and Minister of Planning in the Brazilian government. He spent 1964-1965 at the Economic Growth Center at Yale University and is now Professeur Associé at the Faculté de droit et sciences économiques at the University of Paris. The University of California Press has translated and published two of his earlier books, *Development and Underdevelopment* and *The Economic Growth of Brazil*. In the former the author explains the origins of the industrial economy as the basis of modern Western culture, and analyzes the parallels and divergences of contempororary underdeveloped economies. *The Economic Growth of Brazil* surveys the country's economic history from colonial times to the present, covering the old slave economy in agriculture and mining, the transition to paid labor, and then to an industrial system.

DIAGNOSIS OF THE BRAZILIAN CRISIS

Diagnosis *of the* Brazilian Crisis

BY CELSO FURTADO

TRANSLATED BY SUZETTE MACEDO

UNIVERSITY OF CALIFORNIA PRESS

BERKELEY AND LOS ANGELES 1965

University of California Press
Berkeley and Los Angeles, California
Cambridge University Press
London, England

Dialética do Desenvolvimento, first published in Rio de Janeiro
by Editôra Fundo de Cultura S. A., 1964
Published with the assistance of a grant
from the Rockefeller Foundation
Library of Congress Catalog Card Number: 65-26710
Printed in the United States of America

To my companions of SUDENE,
pilgrims of the Order of Development

REMEMBER

THAT THERE IS NO HAPPINESS

WITHOUT FREEDOM

AND THAT

THE BASIS OF FREEDOM

IS COURAGE.

Pericles' *Funeral Oration to the Athenians*
from Thucydides on *The Peloponnesian War*

Preface

At no time has the responsibility of intellectuals been as great as it is now. And this responsibility has been betrayed by the commissions of some intellectuals and the omissions of others. Scientists, responsible for the manipulation of that supreme creation of the human intellect which is experimental science, have placed themselves at the service of political mythologies against humanity, transforming man's destiny on earth into a simple given element of a political problem to be faced daily, a problem which by its very nature is composed of irrational elements. For his part, the social scientist, whose concern should be to cast some light on the probable consequences of the actions of those responsible for safeguarding the public interest—and possibly to prevent actions that are no less crimes against the community for having been unconsciously carried out—is the great sinner by omission, whether through convenience or cowardice. Not that there exists an intellectual morality above any scales of values, which are necessarily inserted into a given social context. But we cannot fail to recognize that the intellectual has a particular social responsibility, being, as he is, the only element in society who not only can, but should, place himself above the more immediate social conditioners of individual behavior. This permits him to move on a higher plane of rationality and invests him with a very special responsibility: the responsibility of intelligence. Because he has this responsibility, the intellectual cannot refuse to see further than group loyalties or cultural ties allow. His supreme commitment is to the dignity of the human being—an inalienable attribute of the intellectual's very being.

The essays collected in the present volume are the result of an attempt, undertaken from various angles, to grasp the essence of the problem of underdevelopment and to identify the causes of the crisis through which Brazil is passing. My writing, in its fundamental aspects, was carried out in an extremely short space of time: the days that followed the government's attempt to declare a state of emergency in the country in September, 1963. In view of the precipitation of events, which seemed imminent, I felt that the responsibility of the intellectual was more pressing than any other, and once more I was able to verify that it is the force of circumstances that determines the amount of overwork one can impose on oneself.

The first chapter of Part Two, originally written for a non-Brazilian audience, has been included because it provides a background for the analysis presented in the two succeeding chapters.

C. F.

Recife
January, 1964

Contents

Introduction to the American Edition

The present book was written before the military coup d'etat that altered the Brazilian political scene during the last few days of March, 1964. To be more precise, it was prepared between October and December of the previous year, a critical period for the recent political evolution of Brazil. Toward the end of September the Goulart government had made an unsuccessful attempt to declare a state of emergency. This abortive attempt was evidence of the government's awareness of the gravity of the situation. On the other hand, the entire nation was conscious of the fact that the government did not possess the means for coping with a crisis that was daily becoming more acute. Thus a situation arose in which there was a void in power which foreshadowed a change in the conventional methods of political conduct. It was therefore natural that we should have asked ourselves what role should be assigned to the Left during the period of rapid transition through which we were living. It was enough simply to frame the question to realize the extent to which the forces battling for the modernization of Brazil had been overtaken by events. With the intention of promoting an intellectual mobilization of the Left, I wrote the present book, which did not claim to go beyond the formulation of a number of problems concerning which there was scope for a broad exchange of ideas. The heterogeneous nature of the book's contents is due to the diversity of the public to whom it was addressed, a public composed of persons with responsibilities or interests in the numerous political or quasi-political movements aiming toward transforming Brazil from a structurally anachronistic society into a modern nation. For this reason I thought it convenient to open the discussion simultaneously on the theoretical and practical planes. It was necessary to apply critical reasoning to current revolutionary dogmas if we wanted to go beyond the mere repetition of formulas and to exercise political imagination. On the other hand, it was necessary to proceed to an immediate examination of reality, since events were succeeding each other with disconcerting speed. As a matter of fact, this speed was even greater than we had imagined, and our intentions were completely frustrated.

Recent political events in Brazil, far from invalidating the analysis set out in Part Two of the present volume, have only served to confirm the theses there advanced. However, the reader who is unfamiliar with the Brazilian reality may experience some difficulty in attempting to fit the many elements presented in this part of the book into a pattern that would explain the recent aggravation of political instability. In order to facilitate this task, I have undertaken, in this Introduction, to present a broad survey designed to contribute to an understanding of recent events, which occupy a principal place in the minds of all those who concern themselves with the evolution of Brazil.

Brazilian economic development over the last three decades has been a typical case of industrialization directed toward substitution for imports. The expansion of coffee plantations that took place under the stimulus of the high prices prevailing in the late 'twenties led the country into an overproduction crisis at the very moment when the world market was becoming disorganized. Thus the country had simultaneously to face both the external crisis that obliged it to cut imports by half and an internal crisis provoked by the need to finance large surpluses of coffee production. In effect, there were years when the amount of coffee purchased for accumulation or destruction represented as much as 10 percent of the Gross Internal Product. The immediate aim of this policy was, of course, the defense of the coffee-growing interests.

Purchase of surplus coffee financed by expanding the means of payment tended to inflate the money income and to depreciate Brazilian currency abroad, which also favored the coffee growers and coffee merchants, since the price of this product went up in local currency although its international exchange rate was declining. This policy, however, had far wider consequences than were foreseen at the time. In effect, the rapid and persistent depreciation of the currency constituted a powerful protectionist barrier for domestic industry, which began to operate two or three shifts daily with the aid of small additional investments. The profits of the external sector declined, since official backing could only partially compensate for the drop in the real value of exports. Manufacturing production began to attract entrepreneurial capacity and financial resources on a growing scale. In this way, at the same time that the volume of foreign trade was reduced, productive capacity became more diversified. Between 1929 and 1937, while imports declined by 23 percent, industrial output rose by 50 percent.

The most recent phase of Brazilian industrialization is equally illustrative of the disparity between the political objectives aimed at and the results achieved. With a view to defending the international price of coffee, which was threatened by the large stocks still held in Brazil, the Brazilian government, immediately after World War II, followed a policy of external over-valuation of national currency. Experience had demonstrated that devaluation of the cruzeiro would have adverse repercussions on the international price of coffee, leading to a deterioration in the country's terms of trade. This policy, however, had the same effect as a lowering

Whatever may have been the characteristics of the industrialization process, there is no doubt that it entailed consequences for the country's social structure, with important repercussions on the institutions supporting the traditional power system. It would not be out of place to recall that the economic system and social structure of Brazil in 1930 had changed little from the century before. The country's economy continued to be based on the export of a number of tropical products, chiefly coffee, produced on the great estates, and the State continued to finance itself chiefly on the basis of taxes imposed on foreign trade. About four-fifths of the country's population lived on the large estates or was in one way or another subject to the direct authority of the great landowners. Only a small fraction of the population, about 1 percent, participated in the political process. The national state was vaguely identified by the mass of the population through some of its principal symbols. Local offices, even when these were integrated into the federal bureaucracy, were in the hands of the landowners, who held control of the municipal and state governments. In short, those who were in power possessed all the means to keep themselves in power.

Stagnation in the export agricultural sector, concentration of investments in manufacturing activities, and finally the growth of state activities have brought about important changes in the country's social structure over the last three decades. The principal manifestation of change was a process of rapid urbanization. In effect, the Brazilian population, which in 1920 was about 30 million, with about 7 million living in the cities, is today more than 80 million, of whom more than 35 million are concentrated in urban areas, with a much greater proportional growth in medium and large cities. As the urban population represents a much higher coefficient of literacy than the rural, it is natural that political activity should have undergone an important shift in its center of gravity, at least insofar as the electoral process is concerned.

These changes in the social structure did not, however, find any adequate correspondence in the framework of political institutions. The lack of an industrial class, whose position had been defined in terms of a conflict of interests with the basic interests of the former ruling groups, hindered the emergence of a new leadership who could promote the modernization of the institutional framework. Many causes can be found to which to attribute this lack of renewal in Brazilian political leadership, during a period when such important changes were taking place in the country's social structure. I shall draw attention only to the fact that industrialization which begins late in the present century has to create a considerable geographical concentration, in view of the importance of external economies, the need to operate on a basis of large units, the concentration of supplementary services, such as power supply and transport facilities, and so on. Thus, the São Paulo region came to represent an increasing proportion of Brazilian industrial output, and at present contributes approximately 40 percent of this output. This geographical concentration of industrial activity, in a country with a power structure organized on a federal basis, necessarily tends to reduce the political importance of the industrial sector. This circumstance, coupled with the fact that many industrialists also had agricultural interests, contributed toward continuing control of the principal centers of political decision by the leadership connected with the traditional economy.

To the lack of influence on political leadership by the industrial class must be attributed, to a large extent, the slow modernization of the political institutional framework in Brazil. Political constitutions, including the latest (established in 1946), have been a powerful instrument in the hands of the traditionalist oligarchy for preserving its position as the principal political force. The present federal system, in providing considerable power for the Senate, in which the small agricultural states of the most backward areas have a decisive influence, places the legislative power under the control of a minority of the population living in areas where the interests of the great estates hold undisputed sway. On the other hand, as representation of the individual states in the Chamber is proportional to population, illiterates are represented by literate fellow-citizens. Thus, the vote of a citizen living in a State where 80 percent of the population is illiterate is worth five times as much as the vote of a citizen living in a state with one hundred percent literacy. Since the traditional oligarchy is most powerful in the most illiterate areas, the electoral system contributes toward the maintenance of this oligarchy, which finds in illiteracy one of its props. This fact is not without bearing on the strong reaction shown by many local authorities in the more backward regions against the introduction of techniques for simplifying the spread of literacy.

Control of the principal centers of a power system is not a sufficient reason, however, for the majority of the population to accept as legitimate the authority emanating from this control. And it is because this legitimacy has been increasingly lacking in Brazil that the exercise of power by the ruling class has become increasingly difficult. In effect, the relative growth of the urban electorate has offered a permanent challenge to the control of the electoral system by the parties based on the oligarchy. Experience has already shown that, if the creation of new parties is possible, a movement based on the urban centers can decide the results of a major election. In fact, elections of the President of the Republic and State Governors in the more urbanized states have been increasingly influenced by forces that evade control by the oligarchy. Thus conditions had arisen in which the Executive Power represented emergent political forces that defied the control of the Establishment, which concentrates its forces in Congress. Tensions between the two power centers had increased over the last fifteen years, and had on occasion even led to hindrance of government action.[1]

Changes in the Brazilian political process must be analyzed

in the light of the modifications that have taken place in the country's social structure and particularly in the characteristics of its urbanization process. Unlike the classical case observable in Europe during the last century, in which urbanization expressed a rapid change in the occupational structure, for most of the industrial working class in Brazil urbanization has been much more complex. Brazilian industrialization was not accompanied by disorganization of the craft industries, and consequently the first-generation industrial worker was not conscious of having suffered any social degradation. On the contrary, having emerged from conditions similar to those of a rural serf, the worker was aware of having risen in the social scale. However, industrialization was only one of the factors responsible for urbanization. In actual fact, during the decade between 1950 and 1960, while industrial output grew at an annual rate close to 10 percent, employment in industry increased at a rate of 2.8 percent, or approximately half the rate of urban population growth. Increased public expenditure, with a heavy concentration of income creating an expanding market for services, is another factor responsible for the creation of urban employment.

The urbanization process does not constitute, however, a simple reflection of the changes in the country's occupational structure. The underemployed population living in urban areas has actually increased at an even greater speed than the number of people effectively employed in industries and services. This is a phenomenon that is not easy to explain if the country's present agricultural structure is not taken into account. The agricultural pattern that predominates throughout the country, based on rudimentary techniques, has been increasing its costs as a result of the natural exhaustion of soils and the moving of farms further inland from the principal consumption centers along the coast. According to the 1960 census, more than 90 percent of Brazilian agricultural land was situated on medium and large estates utilizing no more than 8 percent of this land for crops. While extreme under-utilization of land continues, as a result of the way in which agriculture is organized, the expansion of the land under cultivation has been dependent to a large extent on multiplying the small estates, whose average size has decreased between 1950 and 1960, according to agricultural census figures for these years. Bearing in mind that this decrease in the average area of the small holding is coupled with soil exhaustion and increased distances from consumption centers, it is not surprising that the standard of living for a great part of the rural population has decreased. This population tends to move to another agricultural region to try to find some form of occupation. From this inter-rural migratory process a growing proportion of the population tends to filter into the urban areas, where even the most precarious livelihood seems attractive compared to the insecurity and extreme poverty of life on the land. In this way, in all Brazilian cities, medium and large, great masses of the underemployed begin to congregate, occasionally being employed in public works, building sites, and unstable jobs in services.

Together with the working class, who are of declining relative numerical importance, and the mass of the underemployed, who are of growing relative importance, the urban population is made up of a substantial and growing contingent of the "middle classes." Here, too, the simple transposition of concepts derived from different historical experiences must be avoided. The middle classes of the classical European model were marked by the presence of the "petit bourgeoisie," who were self-employed and motivated by a strong individualistic spirit, the basis of the Liberal ideology. The present Brazilian middle class is basically made up of white-collar workers, earning medium and high salaries, who work in the numerous government organizations, private banks, offices of industrial and commercial firms, and the various forms of services concentrated in big cities. This middle class is the backbone of the organs of state at their administrative level, the organs of communication, and the cultural institutions. Because they influence movements of opinion and interfere in the organs of decision, these middle-class groups have managed to acquire a series of privileges that range from control of agricultural prices to free higher education for their children. Although intellectually inclined toward the idea of development, and often adopting Leftist positions, the middle classes undoubtedly constitute a privileged group within the present system of income distribution.

This heterogeneous urban population, in which a privileged middle class exists side by side with a growing mass of the underemployed, had become the new decisive factor in Brazilian political struggles. Unlike the happenings in Europe in the last century, where social struggles assumed an increasingly defined form as a conflict between groups with growing class consciousness, which permitted the expression of these conflicts in terms of a political dialogue based on the confrontation of economic interests, in Brazil social tensions express states of dissatisfaction among a growing urban mass difficult to characterize. This amorphous mass is what constitutes the basis for the Populist movements that characterize Brazilian political struggles in recent decades.

In view of this rupture in the basis of the power system, the very principle of legitimacy has been seriously compromised. In order to make itself legitimate, the government must act within the framework of constitutional principles and at the same time fulfill the expectations of the majority responsible for its election. However, in attempting to carry out the substantive mandate of the masses who elected him, the President of the Republic necessarily came into conflict with Congress, and was faced with the alternative of betraying his program or forcing an unconventional way out. In ten years this unconventional way out has included one suicide, one resignation, and one violent deposition. It could be argued that the Presidential candidate could offer a realistic program, taking into account the power of those who control both Congress and a considerable part of the state apparatus.

But this moderate candidate would find it difficult to get himself elected, since another candidate would readily be forthcoming who was prepared to come to terms with the demands of the masses.

The emergence of a mass society, paving the way for Populism, without the formation of new ruling groups able to work out a plan for national development as an alternative to the traditionalist ideology, has been the chief characteristic of the Brazilian historical process in its most recent phase. The Populist leaders, conscious of the psychological state of the masses, called for the country's rapid modernization through "basic reforms" and "structural changes." Control of the principal political power centers, however, continued to be in the hands of the traditional ruling class, who have known how to use Populist pressure as a bogey for bringing to heel the new emergent forces connected with industry and foreign capital. These circumstances, responsible for the growing political instability, favored military intervention and indeed this did in effect take place in March, 1964. The intervention, however, did not eliminate the roots of conflict but only fostered in the old ruling class the illusion of an entrenched security. Now, unless development as a basic aspiration for the Brazilian community is successfully suppressed, social pressures will continue to grow if changes are not introduced into the social structure, and the profundity of these changes will have to increase with the passage of time. A society that shows itself incapable of creating a ruling class equipped to guide its process of change is not necessarily a society that tends to remain stagnant. Nevertheless, there is a high probability that the social cost of such change will increase, if particular historical conditions permit a strengthening of the forces opposed to social change.

C. F.

Yale University
June, 1965

PART ONE
The Dialectic of Development

1

A Return to Dialectics

Hegel's attempt to formulate the principles of a logic of the historical process was the starting point for the most important movement of renewal in social thinking in the nineteenth century.

Hegel established the principle that the world is not made up of ready-made "things" but of a complex of "processes" and that only a logic of development permits us to understand these processes. This logic he described as dialectic. Although in his effort to embrace all human knowledge in a "philosophical system," Hegel gave too wide an application to his dialectic, his point of departure was indubitably the idea of development, arrived at as the result of his careful observation of historical processes. With his dialectic, he attempted both to understand history and to demonstrate the existence of "historical necessity." Each historical period possessed an individual character that gave unity to all its institutions, such as religion, politics, the arts, and so on. A fundamental change in any of these institutions would have repercussions on all the others. These changes, however, did not occur at random but as the result of previous changes and within a logic whose basic principle stressed the fact that historical processes are produced through the conflict of opposites. The dialectical approach allows history to be seen as an opposition of forces in mobile equilibrium. The creative impulse of history resides in the conflict of contradictory forces, but, because there exists a mobile balance of these opposing forces, historical processes present a "meaning." It is from this meaning that Hegel derives his concept of "historical necessity." The fact that Hegel, in his desire to create an all-embracing philosophical system, attempted to find in the progress of an imagined Absolute Idea the basis for his dialectic did not affect its validity as a method. Marx realized this when he said that Hegel had conceived his dialectic standing on its head and that all that he had to do was to turn it right side up again.

The basic difficulties that were encountered by the dialectical method as a working tool in the nineteenth century were the result of two tendencies that had emerged among the Marxist thinkers who used it. The first of these tendencies has its roots in the work of Hegel himself, although it would be difficult to justify from the teachings of Marx: it is the attempt to generalize the use of the dialectical method, applying it to explain natural phenomena. The second of these tendencies, an offshoot of the first, was the result of the desire to transform the dialectic into a set of rules with universal application.

The essence of dialectical thought is the simple idea that the whole cannot be explained by an isolated analysis of its separate parts. The whole is initially perceived as a synthesis, often largely intuitive, made by the human mind, and it is from this synthesis that an analysis of the component parts of the whole acquires its meaning. It does not follow, however, that if the image of the whole is absent, study of the separate parts becomes impossible. Experimental science is precisely the systematic attempt by man to understand the world around him, without using a concept of the whole.

There is no contradiction between dialectics and the conventional methods used in experimental science. For the scientist, however, the dialectical method may be too crude, or even unnecessary. Let us take the case of a paleontologist who is analyzing a fossil to discover the animal to which it belonged. In this case, it is natural to concede that the whole is the animal itself and that the paleontologist can only reach a positive conclusion if, before starting, he possesses a typology of these animals. However, such a typology, which might include not only existing animals but animals that once existed or might have existed, would have been worked out from knowledge of the animals that man was able to study exhaustively by using the conventional methods of science. By carefully analyzing the solar system from those components of the system known to him, Le Verrier was able to infer the existence of an unknown planet. It would be erroneous to suppose, however, that in this case, as in the previous one, there was a preliminary conception of the whole which permitted an understanding of the parts. In fact, the whole —the solar system—was nothing but a hypothesis formulated to explain the behavior of the parts, the starting point for analysis. The explanatory power of this global hypothesis was limited by inadequate knowledge of the parts, and this in turn necessitated the formulation of further hypotheses concerning the parts themselves. The same could be said about the discovery of a substance whose existence was originally inferred from an analysis of Mendeleev's table. Science seeks to understand the behavior of phenomena and to relate these to each other in order to predict similar future behavior. Hypotheses concerning the behavior of a related group of phenomena are often formulated in the guise of a "system." The idea of a system should not be confused with that of the "whole," which is formulated as an image before analytical consideration of the parts. A system can only be identified through an exact definition of a sum total of relationships that creates the interdependence of its parts.

The importance of the dialectical method for an understanding of historical processes derives precisely from the fact that history, at the present stage of man's knowledge, cannot be reconstructed from isolated analyses of the multiple facts that compose it. However, through his individual *praxis*—"the original experience of dialectic," to use an expression of Sartre's [1]—man has intuitively perceived in the historical process that synthetic vision capable of giving unity to multiplicity. It is starting from this original experience that we can speak of dialectics as an instrument for the understanding of historical processes. Lukacs clearly realized this when he affirmed that the central problem of dialectics is a knowledge of the totality of the historical phenomenon.[2] This totalization is a prerequisite for an analysis of the behavior of the parts. In this way the conflict of opposites is only significant as an opposition of the parts to the whole, the whole to the parts, and the whole to itself in the course of a totalization.[3]

The idea of the interdependence of the separate existing institutions of a particular historic period formulated by Hegel derived from the totalizing conception of history. Marx attempted to identify the primary forces that, acting within the whole, provoked the chain of reactions in which the process of historical development presents itself. At the lowest point of this chain, Marx identified the relations of production established among men who live in a society. These relations are a function of the development of the productive forces, i.e., of technology, and constitute in their sum total, the economic structure of society; the other segments of the social structure would be conditioned by this underlying economic structure.[4]

The essence of Marx's hypothesis simply signifies that, of the factors determining a social structure, the most irreducible is the stage of technological development. We are, of course, dealing with a hypothesis formulated at a very high level of abstraction, in which the multiple variables that interfere in the historical process are reduced to only a few elements. It was, however, this daring simplification that allowed Marx to construct the first model for explaining social change, endowing dialectics with an extraordinary effectiveness for the study of historical processes. By presenting social reality as composed of two parts, i.e., the underlying structure made up of the productive forces and the superstructure made up of ideological values, he constructed the most simple of all dialectical models—that in which the whole is composed of only two parts. He repeated this bold simplification when he divided society, for the purpose of analysis, into two classes, with their basic conflict operating as the driving force of the historical process. To what degree these simplifications removed the dynamic model from immediate reality need not concern us here. There is no doubt, however, that they permitted the analysis of history to be undertaken when the social sciences were still at the formative stage.

The attempt at theoretical elaboration by the social sciences in the last decades has been basically directed toward the construction of models that permit a totalizing perception of historical processes, and in this sense, there has been a widespread return to the basic elements of dialectical thought in the form evolved by Marx.

In effect, by placing the concepts of culture and social organization at the center of the concerns of anthropology and sociology, the way was opened for totalizing concepts akin to dialectical modes of thought. As soon as anthropologists realize that the different aspects of a culture are functionally interrelated, the construction of models—instruments for the description and explanation of a sum total of interdependent processes—becomes inevitable, the most simple being those that enable us to construct the dialectical scheme. "The atomizing or isolating treatment of cultural traits," writes Malinowsky, "is regarded as sterile, because the significance of culture consists in the relations between its elements." [5] In attempting to project these interrelationships in time, there was a move toward the formulation of a theory of social change, which led inevitably to the progressive use of dynamic social models. Since the empirical elements available

the sociological constructions of 'maladjustment' or 'adjustment' and all their several synonyms or near-synonyms, where equilibrium is thought of as having a virtual reality in determining the direction of change." [10]

Regardless of the ideological prejudices that inclined social scientists to justify the social status quo (finding in the models of stable equilibrium an ideal instrument), we must recognize that the construction of dynamic models in any field of the social sciences is a task of no mean complexity. In the final analysis, it is a question of defining the conditions under which the multiple variables of a system change from one point of equilibrium to another, as the result of changes in the parameters of this system. Nevertheless, we would still be confined to the realm of what has been called comparative statics, if we limited ourselves to comparing the variables at their two points of equilibrium. The dynamic model would be the model that allowed us to define all the values presented by the variable under observation in its transition from the first position to the final one.

A step forward in the analysis of this complex problem was taken by Myrdal with his model of dynamic social causation. In his observation of the Negro problem in the United States, he verified that the multiple factors involved in the problem are interrelated in a particular way. In order to formulate the problem, he defined a series of relevant variables, such as the level of Negro employment, wages, housing, nutrition, clothing, health, education, stability in family relations, customs, cleanliness, orderliness, trustworthiness, law observance, loyalty to society at large, and so forth. He noted that any movement in one of these variables tended to drag the others in the same direction. What this meant was that any movement of a "Negro variable" in the direction of the "white variables" (a narrowing of the gap between the wages of blacks and whites, for instance) tends to reduce the racial prejudices of the whites, and this reduction acts on all the other "Negro variables" in the direction of the first movement. From this, Myrdal inferred his "Cumulative Principle," according to which any change to a relevant factor in a system makes the system move in a certain direction with a speed dependent on the initial impulse. He affirms that "this concept of a great number of interdependent factors, mutually cumulative in their effects, allows us to overcome the idea of *one* predominant factor, one *basic factor.*" [11] However, it is difficult to see how, without the initial hypothesis of white anti-Negro prejudices, he could have found a solution for his system. In this case there is a *basic factor* and that is race prejudice, which constitutes the original dynamic element and in terms of which it is possible to define the other variables.

Merely identifying the interrelations among the multiple factors that make up a system would be insufficient to construct a dynamic model, that is, to explain a process of development. It will be necessary to introduce some exogenous factor or, in other words, to change one of the structural parameters. There seems to be a general consensus that in modern society this permanently changing parameter is technology. By an accumulative process or a process of circular causation similar to that described by Myrdal, technical innovations set in motion a series of reactions that then reproduce themselves *ad infinitum:* they cause an increase in the average productivity of the system, which in turn leads to a greater availability of goods and services, which in turn leads to new technical advances. In this way, however much we may have advanced in the construction of models, we must recognize that the point of departure for their construction is always some intuitive hypothesis about the behavior of the historical process as a whole. And the most general of these hypotheses is the one offered by the dialectic, where the historic is that which is necessarily in the process of development. The idea of development emerges as a hypothesis for giving an order to the historical process—as the "synthesis of various determinants, unity out of diversity," to quote Marx [12]—from which it is possible to attempt effectively to identify the relations among factors, and to select these factors with a view to reconstructing the process by means of an analytic model.

Because of the high level of abstraction at which it is today possible to construct the model of a historical process, it is only possible to define a limited number of relations involving an even more limited number of variables. As the hypotheses explaining the development process are formulated on the basis of these elementary models, we realize that these hypotheses are truly heroic simplifications. As models with a greater number of variables are evolved, it will become possible to introduce explanatory hypotheses of the process of historical development that can encompass a greater number of concrete situations. A simplifying hypothesis, like that formulated by Marx, dividing the elements that make up the social structure into underlying structures (related to the processes of production) and superstructures (ideological values), was tremendously important as a point of departure for the study of the social dynamic. Up to the present time, this hypothesis has not been replaced by any other with a more effective explanatory power, at the generalized level at which it was formulated. Nevertheless, we must recognize that an analytic model at this level does not have much value as an instrument for practical orientation. And the aim of science is to provide guides for practical action.

2

Economic Development in the Process of Cultural Change

Although the ahistorical nature of modern economic analysis has facilitated the introduction and permitted the improvement of important methodological instruments—the concept of partial and general equilibrium for instance—it has created serious difficulties for placing economic problems in terms of development. In effect, to the extent that the analyst did his best to study conditions of equilibrium based on immediate functional relationships, he rendered himself mentally incapable of grasping economic phenomena *in development* as one aspect of a wider process of social change, the outlines of which can only be seen in the context of a historical reality, i.e., by starting from some figurative image of the social whole and its behavior in time.

The tradition of classical economic thought, since Adam Smith, has been deeply imbued with historical elements. Thus, the Ricardian theory of rent was a logical outcome of the analysis of a class society in which the slowly decomposing feudal elements acted as deadening factors on the process of capitalist development. Starting from these Ricardian hypotheses, Marx formulated a theory of social change applicable to capitalist societies, to which his ideas on economic development are intimately linked. At the heart of these ideas was the concept, directly derived from the Hegelian dialectic, that capitalism as a form of social organization would, *of necessity,* be overcome.

Criticism of the teleological nature of Marx's concept—in which an implicit value judgment of *progress* was distinguished—led to a serious distortion in economic thought. This distortion resulted not only in the removal of historical content from the phenomena that interested economists, but made it almost impossible to understand these phenomena as a *process* within the context of social change.

The reaction against the determinist or teleological nature of the ideas of evolution and progress so dear to the nineteenth century, led to the appearance, in the anthropological field, of the concept of social change. Considering culture as a process in which changes occur in a constant flow, anthropologists began to interest themselves in the factors responsible for these changes, and made detailed studies of the elements most subject to change within a specific culture. These studies not only aroused interest in the *historical* aspects of the social heritage, but also led to a more acute understanding of the interdependence between the different material and non-material elements that go to make up a culture. In addition, the perception of this functional interdependence led to the understanding of culture as a *system* and paved the way for the attempts to apply more perfected analytical instruments for studying the behavior of these systems in the conditioning of hypothetical forms of equilibrium or in the dynamic aspects proper. On the other hand, the introduction of dynamic analytical models for the study of social systems represented for anthropology and sociology the necessary return to economic theory. And for economics it signified the return to historicist ways of thinking.

Social changes basically can be explained in terms of the introduction of innovations that either have an endogenous origin in the culture, or can be regarded as borrowings from other cultures. Since we know that the basic elements of a culture are interdependent in their relationships, we must allow that the introduction of innovations in any of these elements tends to have repercussions on the whole, provoking a series of reactions. These reactions may reestablish, for all practical purposes, the initial values of the basic variables, in which case the existence of a system in stable equilibrium is indicated. Thus, a conflict among the inhabitants of a village may provoke the violent elimination of a leader, who would, however, be automatically replaced, with the original situation thus being to all intents reestablished.

Changes introduced into material culture by technological innovations, however, present peculiar characteristics. These changes are necessarily of a dynamic nature and tend to provoke chain reactions. Take the case of the invention of mechanical weaving. Its introduction into a handicraft society gives rise to a series of reactions both in the organization of production and in the distribution of the social product. The latter reactions, in turn, may have repercussions on the social pattern of the formation of power, which will effect the distribution of the tax burden, the import policy, and so on, a new series of chain reactions in the economic field being thus initiated. In fact, technological innovations, by changing a parameter in the social system, set up a series of readjustments which can be figuratively represented only by means of a dynamic model. If we realize that changes in productive processes resulting from technological innovations are of a dynamic nature (creating situations that render other changes *necessary*), it becomes clear that the best way to represent them is in the form of a *flow* of constant changes in the material culture. And as these changes are translated as an increase in the availability of goods and services to the community, and permit the release of manpower from some sectors and its absorption by others, it is only to be expected that they should affect the whole social structure.

The analysis of the process of change in a cultural system permits the identification of those innovations that do not provoke definite changes in the equilibrium of the system and are therefore absorbed, as well as of those of a typically dynamic nature. Technological innovations introduced into the productive process are included among the latter, and, since they provoke chain reactions in a permanent flow, they condition the whole process of social change. However, as changes in non-material culture (the system of social values) take place at a much slower rate than changes in the productive systems, it is understandable that in periods of rapid absorption of innovations there may be great psychosocial tensions. Marx grasped the essence of this problem when he said that under certain historical conditions, the ideological superstructure can lag behind the development of the productive forces and become a challenge to that development, a situation leading to a period of social revolution.

The validity of the model we have considered—rapid technological changes in the productive processes accompanied by the necessary repercussions on all the other basic elements of a culture—is historically conditioned. Its formulation was based on the study of capitalist economies whose industrialization took place at the beginning of the nineteenth century. In subsequently industrialized capitalist economies (the present phenomenon of underdevelopment), the process of rapid change in the non-material culture often played a major role. The innovations in attitudes and habits absorbed from other cultures provoked, as a rule, a complete change of expectations for important layers of the population, which led to a series of chain reactions affecting the whole social structure. However, once changes in the productive system had started, the resultant chain reaction led to a new pattern that tended to approximate the model previously referred to.

Although the concept of social change was introduced by anthropologists and sociologists in their anti-evolutionist concern to remove any meaning from history, the Hegelian concept of a historical process moving in a certain necessary direction, taken over by Marx together with dialectics, is in some ways given new life in the theory of economic development as one particular aspect of the process of social change. In fact, we must define economic development as *a process of social change by which a growing number of human needs—either those already in existence or those created by the change itself—are satisfied by means of differentiation in the productive system resulting from the introduction of technological innovations.* Science plays a strategic role in this process, since technological innovations emerge from its progress. But, as the advance of science is related to economic development, i.e., the greater availability of goods and services, it is perfectly possible that, in certain historical circumstances, such as those existing today, conditions will be created for the progressive advance of science, with prospects for the renewed economic development of a particular society.

The introduction of innovations into a culture is not effected without arousing resistance to them, and this resistance often expresses itself in social conflict. The conflict results from the conscious search, by the members of a society, for values which are mutually exclusive. In the search for these values, rival individuals or groups make use of the most varied weapons, ranging from violence to persuasion, from terror to ridicule.

It is a currently observable fact that innovations introduced into the superstructure of values arouse greater reactions, provoking sharper conflicts, than those that penetrate into the productive system. In fact, as a result of the decentralization of the latter in capitalist economies, the introduction of innovations has, at first, a limited effect. Thus, the production of a new article or the introduction of a new process at first appears as an isolated fact with unforeseeable consequences.

The interests initially opposed may be limited or difficult to identify. It is at the stage of widespread diffusion of the innovation that these begin to manifest themselves. The new product might provoke a lowering of income in some distant agricultural area, or the new process might lead to a certain amount of unemployment. However, because of the complexity of economic activity, the conflicts resulting from either of these innovations will be mixed up with others, and the final causes will be difficult to determine.

In societies in which private ownership of the means of production predominates, conflicts resulting from the introduction of innovations into the productive process tend to transform themselves into conflicts of social classes. As the diffusion of innovations aggravates competition among producers, the struggle for survival calls for rigorous supervision of production costs, that is to say, it exerts pressure on wages or provokes unemployment. In this way, although the competition is *among producers,* its final effects are translated into conflicts between the owners of the means of production and the wage earners. By becoming aware of the fact that the objectives they are seeking are mutually exclusive, since there is a division of the product, the two groups tend to achieve a growing inner articulation and to transform themselves into classes organized for the struggle that in capitalist societies assumes decisive significance in the social process.

The introduction of a technological innovation, by the very fact that it tends to increase the product, creates a surplus that the community can use either to increase its productive capacity or to improve immediately its social welfare Where private ownership of the means of production prevailed, the ruling classes sought to retain the surplus for themselves, wholly or in part, incorporating it into the process of capital formation as a means of increasing their own power. The division of society into classes with mutually exclusive interests was a necessary result of the formation of capital which is at the root of the historical process of economic development. If primitive forms of community organization with collective ownership had prevailed, the possibilities for an accumulation of capital would have been much more limited. The forms of social organization that, in the long run, permitted a more rapid accumulation of social wealth and therefore a greater offensive and defensive power for the community, have prevailed.

The class struggles engendered by the social division of wealth which proved to be the most effective—appropriation by a minority of the means of production—reflect the growth of consciousness on the part of individual groups of the antagonism of their interests. Since the conflicts underlying this class struggle result from the very mechanism of appropriating the surplus that permits the growth of productive capacity, it would be wrong to suppose that it withers economic development of a society. The acute psychosocial tensions that characterize pre-capitalist economies in the phases of transition to capitalist economies result much less from the class struggle itself, than from the pressure exerted by this struggle for the more rapid elimination of outgrown cultural patterns with no functional relation to the capitalist system of production. The forms of social organization thus challenged correspond to a system of interests created with no basis in the new economic reality. And the defense of these interests tends to be all the more intense as its agents are unable to achieve any subjective understanding of the new social reality in the process of evolving, and in which they will have no place.

Technological innovations, which are the essence of economic development, do not simply provoke changes in the structure of the productive system. They provoke, as we have indicated, a series of chain reactions resulting from the interdependence existing among the basic elements of the culture as a whole. Thus, changes in the economic structure tend to bring with them changes in the whole social structure. This happens not as a simple cause and effect, but in terms of certain historical conditions. In so-called underdeveloped economies, this process of adjustment of the social structure to the flux of changes resulting from the assimilation of a new technology presents a series of peculiarities that distinguish it from the current model of capitalist development.

The developed capitalist economy of our time can be seen as a socioeconomic system with a relative aptitude for maintaining itself in dynamic equilibrium. The advance of science, which appears as an exponential function of economic development itself, assures a permanent advance in technology. In this way, the growth of capital flows along previously opened channels, coming up only against those institutional obstacles stemming from insufficient or tardy adjustments to the institutional framework that disciplines the different economic streams. The chief of these obstacles reflects the persistence of anachronistic forms in the distribution of incomes, which is expressed in terms of a lack of vigor in the final demand for consumption or investment. The introduction into capitalist economies of mitigated forms of planning aims to eliminate these obstacles by correcting, through fiscal policy or in other ways, the anachronisms in the distribution of income, and increasing by means of multiple analyses of the relationships among the relevant variables, the capacity of the investors to recognize the expectations of the consumers and to predict their probable future behavior. In some cases, this mitigated planning has been limited to clarifying certain decisions, permitting a higher degree of rationality.

At other times, the planning authorities have diagnosed inflexibility in the economic structure, and have attempted to remove obstacles by undertaking a partial reallocation of investments.

In present underdeveloped economies—i.e., in those that absorb technological innovations almost entirely by borrowing—the adaptation of social structures becomes a more complex problem. The use of new techniques in the productive system disorganizes a layer of the existing handicraft economy and immediately creates a problem of surplus manpower with no possibilities of absorption. This surplus flows back into artisanal forms of subsistence economy creating a duality in the economic system that conditions the whole of the subsequent social process. The dualism of the economic structure is reflected, on the one hand, in an extremely unequal distribution of income, and, on the other, in a weak demand for the final product. In effect, the appropriation of the surplus by ruling groups meets no resistance from the workers, whose class-consciousness is only slowly formed as a result of the widespread underemployment created by the dualism of the system. This absence of vigor among the class of wage earners is also a factor handicapping the growth of an internal market. In this way, the surplus in the hands of the ruling classes tends to give rise to forms of luxury consumption, or to filter out of the country as foreign investment.

3

Class Struggles in the Development of Political Institutions

We have noted how the patterns of social organization that proved the most effective came to predominate. They precipitated the formation of social classes with antagonistic interests, and the recognition of these antagonisms led to the various forms of class struggle that history records. It was in this that Marx found the original driving force of the historical development process. In his model, the level of technology, and the consequent relationships of production, determined the social structure of a certain historical stage through a series of actions and reactions. However, what gives the historical process its dynamic character is the fact that these elements of the underlying structure are in a state of permanent change; this change is the result of social conflicts created by a productive process based on private appropriation of the means of production. The importance of social conflicts in the process of introducing innovations and diffusing new values through a culture, is today universally recognized by students of the social dynamic. On the other hand, there is also agreement in the social sciences that the forms of division of labor are projected as schemes of social stratification, the most universal of these being the division of society into classes. Marx's hypothesis was inferred from the observation of a capitalist society at a certain stage of development, although the generalized way in which it was initially formulated in the *Communist Manifesto* led to the attribution of a false universality for the hypothesis. Engels' ideas on the origin of the state, relating this solely to the class struggle, equally contributed to the disorientation of students of the subject.

The importance of the class struggle in the development of industrial capitalism derives from certain characteristics peculiar to its social structure. The difference between industrial capitalism and all previous forms of economic organization is that the former gave rise to a productive system in which large productive units predominate, and in which these units tend to cluster in an attempt to cut production costs. The most important social consequence of this form of organizing production has been urbanization. The old market-city, with its heterogeneous floating population, has been replaced by the industrial metropolis, with great masses of wage earners subject to periodic unemployment. These were the specific conditions that permitted the growth of class-consciousness, without which it would have been impossible to transform occasional group conflicts into an organized class struggle. If we compare the situation of the industrial working class with that of the peasants in the nineteenth century, the nature of the problem becomes clear.

The peasants, like industrial workers, have their *raison d'être* in the private appropriation of the means of production, and their interests are in this case in obvious conflict with those of the landowners. However, their struggle against the landowners never became a basic factor in the development of modern society, and it cannot be said that the peasants achieved a state of full class-consciousness. The development of the productive forces did not act as an aggravating factor in the antagonism between peasant and landowner, but simply created new forms of employment of increasing importance outside the rural areas; this led to a split in the class owning the means of production. The antagonism between the two branches of the proprietary classes,

non among many other forms of social conflict, into a factor of extreme importance. For the first time, the principal driving force in the historical process ceased to be conflict among factions of the dominating class belonging to the same or different political groups, and became a struggle engendered by the social organization itself. We are dealing, therefore, with a society subject to much greater internal instability than previous societies, and this instability is expressed in terms of intensified political activity, calling for the participation of much broader segments of the population. The role of the state in this new type of society becomes extremely important.

To go deeper into the subject we must abandon Hegel's starting point with its marked distinction between civil society and state. Hegel idealized the state and removed from it all its common functions as an agent for rendering services, functions that he imagined could be exercised by an organized civil society. Now, it would not be easy to imagine a society organized to apply the rule of law, even of private law, without the existence within that society of a constraining force, which is the same thing as a state. From the moment when society has grown sufficiently for its members to need to regulate conduct by means of general rules which must be enforced by an authority that does not derive its legitimacy from family ties, we are faced with an embryo political organization; whether we call it a civil society or a state becomes irrelevant. What concerns us is the recognition that any social structure that has reached a certain degree of differentiation needs to organize itself politically in order to prevent its inner conflicts from destroying it. It is important to bear in mind the nature *sui generis* of political organization, the instrument which society uses to discipline itself, which may exercise its monopoly of armed force in the name of the community as a whole. The existence of armed forces and public servants is the outward manifestation of this political organization, at the peak of which are the ruling elements that constitute the link between the state-machine and the politically organized society. Political power is, indeed, based precisely on this link: it is *legitimized* by the fact that the community sees in those who exercise it the arbiters of their interests, and it is rendered *effective* because those who hold it control the state-machine. Power without a minimum of legitimacy can only be maintained by terror, as during the foreign occupation of a country, and without a minimum of effectiveness it has a very slight chance of survival. If the state existed as a simple instrument for the oppression of a minority class, even if it reached a high level of efficiency, it would have only a slender chance of survival. Marx himself made this observation about the French State on the eve of the Revolution, when the bourgeoisie and the masses denied it any legitimate right to represent their interests.

As the most powerful organization within a society, it is perfectly natural that the state should come to play, in many cases, an autonomous role in the conflicts that distinguish the development of that society. This happened during the long struggles that characterized the birth pangs of the modern European national states. The most powerful political organizations, represented by the monarchies, served as arbiters (in their own interests) in the conflict between the feudal aristocracy and the bourgeoisie. Engels recognized this fact when he stated: "There are periods when the conflicting classes draw so close to an equilibrium that the power of the state acquires, as the apparent mediator, a certain momentary independence vis-à-vis each class." [4] And he proceeds to quote as examples the absolute monarchies of the seventeenth and eighteenth centuries, the two Bonaparte regimes, and "Bismarckism." However, the exceptions turn out to be more numerous than the rule.

The development of industrial capitalism in the nineteenth century affected existing political organizations in two ways. On the one hand, the greater internal social instability, resulting from the class struggle, called for the creation of much more flexible political structures so that power could retain the required minimum of legitimacy. On the other hand, the growing wealth of the society greatly increased community needs, which called for an unprecedented growth of the state apparatus in order to provide services. Modern democratic regimes are the result of the convergent action of these two forces.

It is perfectly understandable that the relative neutrality of the state, the most important of the political institutions, when confronted by conflicts among individuals and groups of individuals, should have become seriously compromised from the moment when these conflicts, now transformed into class struggles, began to divide society as a whole. In effect, when the great conflicts of antagonistic classes emerged with the development of industrial capitalism, political power acquired a completely new importance. The struggle for power, hitherto a matter of dynastic rivalry, began to interest increasingly varied groups. Everywhere, evolution was in the direction of creating political institutions that were sufficiently flexible for the growing masses of the population to participate in the formation of power. Whether under a monarchical regime or a republic, parliamentary governments were organized capable of representing the interests of increasingly important layers of the population. Without this flexibility of political institutions, the class struggle could not have played the role of driving force in the development of the productive powers that it came to play, nor could capitalism have developed at the rate it did. Engels realized the nature of the problem when he affirmed that "the Democratic Republic is the only form of State in which the final struggle between the proletariat and the bourgeoisie can take place." [5] The idea that class struggles could be avoided by concentrating all power in the hands of the bourgeoisie and creating a totalitarian state appeared much later, when capitalism saw itself threatened by the first successful proletarian revolution. During the nineteenth century, political institutions evolved in the direction of democratization of the sources of power to meet the needs of a rapidly developing capitalist economy.

The second basic aspect of the transformation of political institutions as the result of the advance of industrial capitalism, was the effect that the rapid increase of national wealth had on the functions of the State. It is surprising that Marx, usually so acute in his analyses of historical processes, did not grasp the true nature of this phenomenon. In a famous passage from his *Eighteenth Brumaire,* he gave a detailed outline of the exorbitant growth of the French bureaucratic machine. He attributed this growth, however, to the bourgeoisie's need to defend itself by increasingly powerful means. This "horrible parasitic organism that was wound like a thread round the body of French society," was, however, one of the consequences of the changes that were taking place in the social structure as a result of the development of the productive forces. The progressive diffusion of education, the public services required by the growth of towns, the administration of the substructure related to new methods of communication and transportation, and numerous new functions, all fell to the state, and this required the creation of an expanding and ever more complex organization. The interesting thing, however, is that this enormous organization tends to become, in a society divided into classes, an autonomous strata of that society, with aspirations and attitudes that are not always those of the classes in conflict, even if the state is to a large extent the instrument of one of these classes. Thus, a new factor for political stability is created by means of the growing specialization of the state-machine, whose simple outward control no longer signifies changes of great consequence. Max Weber observes that "a highly organized bureaucracy is one of the most difficult social organizations to destroy," and adds, "Where bureaucratization of a regime was taken to its final extremes, a practically unbreakable form of power relationships was created." [6] The process of bureaucratization does not involve simply the growth of the state apparatus, it also involves important qualitative changes in political procedure. The element of improvisation in certain public functions, previously based on subjective criteria or simply the interests of groups, was gradually replaced by the impersonal agent, acting within a scheme division of labor subject to more widely applicable and supposedly rational criteria. Thus did bureaucratization permit an extraordinary increase in the *effectiveness* of those in power, which in turn opened up the possibility of maintaining power at decreasing levels of *legitimacy*.

If the class struggles constituted the basic driving force of development in societies with an industrial capitalist economy, we should ask whether this struggle tended to become intensified or to slacken with the development of capitalism. During the first half of the nineteenth century, when political institutions had not yet adapted themselves to the capitalist dynamic, class struggle was expressed in powerful political tensions that were occasionally transformed into revolutionary processes. However, after the middle of the century and particularly during the last quarter, social evolution in Europe took a different direction. Political institutions became increasingly more open to the participation of the working class, organized into political parties, and social conflicts began to express themselves chiefly in syndical terms. There is no evidence, however, that these conflicts diminished either in this period or later. The only known attempt to operate a capitalist economy with the total elimination of class conflict was made by fascism. Everything indicates that this type of political organization would necessarily tend to destroy the dynamism of the capitalist system, and be faced with effects of prolonged stagnation in a society divided into antagonistic classes. This tendency was avoided by the fascist regimes of the thirties by increasing state participation in the national means of production with a view to rearmament and other forms of expanding state action. However, this type of policy could not be taken very far without compromising the very bases of the capitalist system. In the more developed capitalist economies, class struggle began to take new forms; the earlier spontaneous actions and sporadic movements were replaced by the technique of pressure groups who kept up a permanent activity, strategically directed. The democratic regime is precisely that which permits the full development of these divergent tendencies and opens the way for resolving the conflicts resulting from them. In the words of a well-known American political sociologist: "A stable democracy requires the manifestation of conflict or cleavage so that there will be struggle over ruling positions, challenges to parties in power, and shifts of parties in office." [7] The fact that we affirm that the modern democratic state is far from being solely the power for repression at the service of one class that Engels refers to, does not imply ignorance of the currently observable truth that the basic mission of this state is to assure the maintenance of the status quo. And the principal component of this status quo is a group of institutions created to perpetuate a series of privileges belonging to a social minority that controls the means of production. The development of democratic society was in the direction of a progressive elimination of those privileges that operated antisocially—that is to say, that held back the expansion of the productive forces and so deadened social development. Agrarian reform, for instance, was everywhere undertaken in this spirit. The same can be said of fiscal and other measures of the state that interfere with private enterprise in an attempt to assure and maintain the level of employment, and to avoid losses incurred by cyclic depressions. Thus, the specific characteristic of the capitalist democratic state is not really a tendency to eliminate privileges. On the contrary, privileged groups can flourish and maintain power. Its essential characteristic is the tendency to eliminate those privileges that hold up the development of the productive forces. This is the reason it should be open to the action of all groups who are involved in the productive process and who seek to increase their share of income, either through open competition or by exerting organized pressure on the labor market. The institutional framework should therefore be sufficiently flexible to adapt itself whenever pressure generated by conflict reaches the point where social intercourse becomes impossible. The impulse for this permanent reform is the general agreement that a social interest above groups and classes does exist, and this social interest is guided by the development of the productive forces.

We should ask to what extent the complex of privileges that exists at the core of the capitalist economy is a necessary condition for the functioning of a pluralistic democratic society, which is, without question, of all the societies hitherto known, the one in which the individual creative personality is most free to act. We are faced here with a problem of the highest political importance. A great deal of thought has been devoted to the fact that no society that has succeeded in eliminating class privileges based on private ownership of the means of production has, at the same time, succeeded in organizing itself as a genuine and stable democracy, that is, one that allows the political organization of groups disagreeing with those currently in power.

At first glance, since the state is *inter alia* a repressive force designed to preserve a structure of privileges, once these have been eliminated with the extinction of the exploiting class, the characteristics of a repressive force should gradually disappear. This theory is based on the idea that in bourgeois society, the limitations of freedom are the result of the need to defend the privileges of the class owning the means of production. However, this does not seem to be true, since, as we have already indicated, the reason for the spread of freedom in democratic capitalist societies was their growing institutional stability. The cycle of revolutions directly caused by the class struggle in western Europe came to an end in the third quarter of the last century. This institutional stability is due to the existence of a powerful class which owns the means of production and has wide interests to defend. Just as the existence of a class conditioned to increase its share of the product, i.e., the industrial worker, gives a tremendous dynamism to capitalist society, so the survival in this society of another class that has created broad interests is responsible for its institutional stability. If we pause to analyze these facts, we will see that only by means of a dynamic model will it be possible to understand the interrelations between these apparently divergent forces. As long as the system continues to grow, it is possible to avoid an aggravation of class conflict by meeting the demands of the workers without fundamentally compromising privileges. In this case, we must conclude that the progress of civil liberties in bourgeois societies was the result, less of the active participation in political decisions by the working class, than of the confidence the capitalist class gained within a framework of flexible political institutions.

We must now ask: What degree of stability can a classless society achieve at the present level of development of the productive forces? Who will decide whether to produce steel or boots? Who will plan for the planners?

As Marx so well said in one of his famous theses on Feuerbach: *the educator himself needs to be educated.* Since there is no significant interest group in a classless society, the possibility of maintaining a coherent political line could be reduced to a critical point, thus causing permanent social instability. The non-existence of privileges does not signify that the desire for privileges has disappeared. To seek a solution to this problem was the task before the "dictatorship of the proletariat," and not only the task envisaged by Lenin.

In formulating his idea of "the dictatorship of the proletariat," Marx had in mind the necessity for drastic action with a view to shattering the state-machine that had so appalled him during the French civil wars of the mid-nineteenth century. The experience of the 1871 Commune seemed to him a clear indication that society possessed the means to organize itself *democratically* almost instantly, once the class structure has been destroyed. In 1917, Lenin continued to think that the basic task of the social revolution was to *demolish* the ready-made state-machine. However, he presumed that this demolition would be a rapid process and that it would not hit the bureaucratic machine, as such, but only its peak. This was a far cry from the Saint-Simonian myth incorporated into the *Communist Manifesto* according to which "the government of men would be replaced by the administration of things," but it still preserved the illusion that the new tasks of the state could be carried out by anyone, or by technicians paid "a worker's wage," as they were during the Commune. "Once the capitalists have been eliminated," said Lenin, "once the resistance of the exploiters has been overcome by the armed workers and the bureaucratic machinery of the present state has been broken—we will have a mechanism freed of its parasites, a mechanism admirably equipped from the technical point of view, one which the armed workers can easily set in motion by contracting technicians, supervisors, and accountants and paying them a worker's wage." [8]

Experience proved, however, and Lenin before his death recognized, that the task to be carried out by the "dictatorship of the proletariat" went much further than the simple elimination of the exploiting class and the demolition of the ready-made bureaucratic machine of state. The question then asked was whether this task would ever end. The same problem appeared a generation later, when in Central Europe other societies basing their organization on public ownership of the means of production arose. However, the naïve prophecy of Engels, whose last book ended with the affirmation that once class conflict had been eliminated in the new society, production would be organized on the basis of "a free and equal association of the producers," continued alive in the minds of all socialists as the highest of ideological aspirations.

As Mannheim acutely observed in his analysis of the Soviet experience, the task to be carried out consisted of "overcoming three types of difficulty: how to create a new group of leaders who would guarantee a stable social order, how to find factors that could identify social status, not based on income and property, and how to offer new incentives for work." [9] In fact, the problem was to establish social stability without basing it on a structure of existing economic interests. This proved possible only by maintaining an extraordinary missionary zeal among a large group of leaders, and creating a complex bureaucratic edifice based on the state, the trade unions, and the Communist Party. Max Weber's theory that "complete bureaucratization creates power relationships which are practically unbreakable," was thus confirmed.

The effort to create a stable social structure not based on the elements traditionally serving to maintain this stability, entailed the submission of all political activity to rigorous discipline. This strictness naturally had to be presented as a temporary measure, with the justification that there was much more to demolish than Lenin had originally supposed. However, the Soviet experiment, like the Chinese—in which the disturbing threat of foreign intervention was not present as a major factor—indicates that the roots of the problem go much deeper. If we consider the evolution of modern political institutions, we see that progressive consolidation of so-called civil liberties has been intimately linked to the general development of industrial capitalist societies. In fact, the ideology of natural law in the form of the liberal doctrine of "laissez-faire" was the rationalization (the ideological justification) of the social organization that suited free enterprise economy. As an eighteenth century ideologist so well said, "business breathes liberty." The words "liberty and equality" were always inscribed on the battle flags of the bourgeoisie, equality meaning equality before the law that sanctioned the privileges of the bourgeoisie. This law, as Anatole France ironically remarked, *equally* forbade both the pauper and the millionaire to sleep under bridges.

However, these formal liberties were an important point of reference for the demands of the politically rising working class, who attacked the bourgeoisie with the ideas of the latter. On the other hand, the development of industrial capitalism called for provision to be made for the class struggle, involving the working class in political activities. Since the political advances of the workers meant, in the final analysis, freedom to challenge the privileges of the ruling class, capitalist development helped create a society increasingly open to individual action. This is why, even where a powerful oligarchy remained in power supported by a monarchical regime, as in the case of Germany, there was tremendous progress in consolidating civil liberties. In fact, Lenin could refer to Germany in 1902 as "a politically free country." [10]

We must now ask if, once the necessary social stability has been achieved, Soviet society can move toward a greater flexibility in the power structure, a necessary condition for reestablishing genuine civil liberties. In the first place, we must bear in mind that development of a society with a centrally planned economy does not depend on tensions created by groups or classes with conflicting interests. Development depends, quite simply, on the attitude of that society toward its own destiny, expressed through the organs that represent the community. In the Soviet case, this problem has been simplified because of the challenge offered by the need to create a material basis, and consolidate military power, in the initial stages of development, and later by the competition for world leadership, the space race, and so on. What should be pointed out is that development, in this type of society, becomes increasingly dependent on the clear formulation of the community's aspirations, and that the social structure must be organized in such a way that the constant up-dating of these aspirations becomes feasible. To what degree it will be possible to reconcile rigid planning of the underlying cultural structure (the material basis) with a certain pluralism in the gestation process of non-material values in the culture, is a question that only experience will answer. What immediately concerns us is whether there are effective internal forces working to create more opportunity for individual action.

The basic problem, in Marx's own terms, is to determine who are the educators and who is to educate them. In this case the educators are those operating the system, giving the state the effectiveness without which it could not survive. The operators are precisely that great bureaucratic machine that gave Soviet society its stability, and that plays the same stabilizing role as that played by the class owning the means of production in the bourgeois democracies. And who will undertake the role of challenging the establishment, which in bourgeois societies has been played by the workers? The problem is not, as many socialists influenced by Marx's reflections on the Commune have thought, to give a *democratic organization* to the state-machine. No one today doubts that any society, at our present level of technological development, needs to base itself on a complex bureaucratic apparatus to fulfill the aims of its own development. Society, in eliminating classes with antagonistic interests, has reduced the area of conflict, or has eliminated from this area such fundamental problems as those related to the formation of capital and the distribution of income. But we cannot therefore deduce that it will be sufficient to organize the population along democratic lines for these problems to be wisely considered with full awareness of their importance. This important work of renewal and of defining the community's aspirations is being undertaken, within limits, by the class of so-called "intellectual workers" in Soviet society. Because of their unavoidably pluralist organization, the intellectuals, to a large extent have escaped the bureaucratizing tendency that predominates in any society where stability is not directly based on a structure of privileges. Since it is their role to interpret values in all fields of culture, the intellectuals are very well placed for identifying the aspirations that express the deepest trends in social feeling. However, for this type of influence to have any real effect on a society in which power is basically bureaucratic, tremendous material development would be required. During the intermediate phase, when scarcity is closer than abundance, and when the fruits of labor have to be distributed in a very unequal way, the bureaucratic apparatus has every chance of preserving its absorptive influence on the centers of power. The paths to freedom through social revolution have been, up to the present time, long and painful.

4

Class Ideologies in the Struggle for Power

In order to understand the socialist movement, we must remember that it emerged from the experience of class struggle, and that its doctrinal formulation is chiefly the result of the intellectual effort of men who took part in it. In one of his famous theses on Feuerbach, Marx calls attention to the need to observe the sensible world through *concrete human activity* such as *practice*.[1] And he says that revolutionary activity is practical critical activity. It is from this point that we should start when approaching the problem of revolution in the development of societies based on industrial capitalism. We have already observed that the first and greater part of the nineteenth century was marked by a series of revolutions in western Europe, with France as the center of radiation. Without going into a detailed analysis of this subject, we can admit that the instability of French society, still suffering from the traumatic effects of the Revolution and the Napoleonic Wars, is to a large extent responsible for these convulsions. At the root of the struggle was the dispute for power between groups of the legitimate or usurping nobility, and the "grande bourgeoisie," which had begun to break up into different sectors. There is no doubt, however, that this instability also reflected institutional tensions, provoked by the growth of an industrial economy based on the great mass of workers situated in a handful of cities. We have already observed that class struggle played a major role in the social system that arose with the Industrial Revolution. The mass unemployment caused by economic crises, the strikes that paralyzed part of the productive system, and other equally unwanted phenomena, provided severe tests for the institutional framework, and required of the political leadership a new virtuosity for which the apprenticeship had only just begun. In short, it was a period in which the most significant adjustments introduced into the social structure were the result of revolutions and near revolutions.

It is from the practical critical activity of the intellectuals of this period that revolutionary socialist thought emerged. In Marx, for instance, the activity of the revolutionary always cleared the way for the thinking man, although the activity of the latter illuminated a field very much broader than that in which the former moved. It is necessary to bear this in mind in order to understand the discrepancy between Marx's ideas on revolution and his general concept of the development of capitalist economy. In 1848, when the revolution broke out in Paris and spread through Europe, Marx seriously believed that he was witnessing the birth of a great new revolutionary process that would stop only when bourgeois domination had been eliminated. As Engels observed in a calm analysis made many years later "History proved that we were wrong." And he added: "It clearly demonstrated that the state of economic development on the continent at that time was not, by a long way, ripe for the removal of capitalist production." [2]

Marx's hypothesis can be summarized as follows: the final cause of the revolution was the economic crisis beginning in 1847, and even if its intensity diminished as the result of the return of prosperity, it would recur when there was a new crisis. Starting from the irrefutable fact that crises were recurrent, and postulating the probability of their becoming worse, in view of what was happening in 1848, Marx supposed that the decline of capitalist economy had set in and that the first step in this decline was the spread of revolution everywhere. The important role played by the Paris working class in this revolution supported his theory. The revolution that Marx was thinking of at the time was far from the model he later developed and outlined in his Preface to the *Contribution to the Critique of Political Economy*. In the latter model, the disappearance of the bourgeoisie would be a consequence of its social uselessness at a stage when society would be practically divided into two classes. The 1848 Revolution had not been started by the industrial workers, but on the initiative of minority groups who had infiltrated into the state-machine and managed to arouse the popular *masses,* who were more or less ignorant of the objectives in view. Referring to the petty bourgeoisie that made up the majority of the urban population, Engels described it as "extremely important in any political body and in all modern revolutions." [3] In an extremely lucid analysis, Engels gives us a clear idea of how he and Marx saw the revolutionary process in this initial stage. "All revolutions of modern times," he says, "have shown certain characteristics that seemed inseparable from every revolutionary struggle, and these seemed to us equally applicable to the struggles of the proletariat for its emancipation." [4] And he tells us that these characteristics in each case involved the displacement of one ruling class by another, and that these ruling classes were always small minorities taking over the state apparatus and remodelling institutions in accordance with their own interests. What characterized the new ruling group was that it was "able to rule and qualified to do so by the degree of economic development" which put it in a position either to attract the support of the majority, or to secure their passive acceptance. The essential point, however, is that revolutions were always "revolutions of minorities." In this case, why not admit that once a certain revolutionary situation had been created, a minority group could take power in the service of the working class and later obtain the support of the masses? Engels asks: "Because the masses would be less susceptible to ideas which were the truest reflex of their economic position. . . ?" [5]

The revolutionary model we have just summarized is based on extremely simple ideas: revolution is always the result of a minority effort, and the masses will support that minority if it is able to stay in power and if its actions satisfy the desire for social development. This model, however, can explain a revolution that has already started but says nothing about the factors that create the pre-revolutionary situation. On this, Marx's position seemed to be as follows. Economic crises are inevitable, will become increasingly acute, and will be responsible for the creation of a pre-revolutionary situation. Capitalist development in the second half of the nineteenth century was in this respect, however, disappointing. There were crises, but they did not produce the expected aggravation. The bourgeoisie, because of fear or cunning, gradually permitted more changes in the political institutions which placed the working class in a position of equal responsibility at the center of decision. At the end of the last century, the working-class party in Germany accounted for a quarter of the registered voters. Economic development, by bringing with it a constant increase in national wealth, created the conditions for satisfying the claims of the working classes, without altering the basic structure of the regime.

During this period Marx continued his tireless research and gave much greater depth to his analysis of the development of capitalism. In his most lucid text on the subject he wrote: "At a certain stage of their development the material forces of production in a society come into conflict with the existing relations of production . . . which from forms of development of the forces of production turn into their fetters. Then occurs a period of social revolution. With the change of the economic foundation the entire immense superstructure is more or less rapidly transformed." [6] The social revolution is therefore a phenomenon characterizing a period, and the speed with which it takes place can only be determined by historical conditions. Nothing prevents it from taking as much *time* to progress as did the Industrial Revolution. Apparently with reference to this point, Marx added: "No social order ever disappears before all the productive forces for which there is room in it have been fully developed." [7] Along the same line, Engels wrote: "The time of surprise attacks, of revolutions carried through by small conscious minorities at the head of the unconscious masses, is past. Where it is a question of a complete transformation of the social organization, the masses themselves must cooperate, must themselves already have grasped what is at stake, why they are intervening (with their bodies and their lives). The history of the last fifty years has taught us that. But in order that the masses may understand what is to be done, long and persistent work is required." [8]

The renewal of revolutionary thought with Lenin consisted basically of a return to Marx's position of 1848. This change is perfectly understandable as Russia at the beginning of the twentieth century was no different from western Europe at the beginning of the nineteenth, since its social and political development was much slower.

Lenin's ideas were always directed strictly toward action, making them highly effective in meeting the concrete conditions that had originally engendered them. But they seemed too narrow to western European observers. Probably referring to his western critics, Lenin said: "Those who under absolutism want a broad organization of workers with elections, reports, universal suffrage, et cetera., are simply incurable Utopians." [9] Lenin's ideas were simple and direct, generally taken from western Marxist thinkers but used in a specific sense. Thus, from Kautsky he took the idea that the working class is unable to form an independent ideology for itself. "The socialist conscience is an element imported from outside for the class struggle and not something that develops spontaneously," wrote Kautsky in a passage cited by Lenin.[10] This ideology is a more ample creation of society based on knowledge of economics and other sciences, and its elaboration is principally the work of intellectuals. Left to itself, the working class tends to fall into the snare of bourgeois ideology, "which is in all respect the most polished and possesses *immeasurably* greater means of diffusion." [11] The maximum that the working class can spontaneously create is a syndicalist mentality. This being so, the existence of a party to spread socialist ideology among the workers becomes necessary. And in the conditions prevalent in Russia, thought Lenin, this party would have to be composed of professional revolutionaries. His concern, therefore, was wholly for the formation of this party which was to have the double function of propagating socialist ideology (Marxism) among the workers, and struggling against the state-machine with the final aim of destroying it. "The professional art of the revolutionary," he affirmed, "is the struggle against the political police." [12]

In formulating the revolutionary doctrine that he adhered to strictly right up to the end, Lenin was in the same frame of mind as Marx was in 1848. The criticism made of him, that he deviated from genuine Marxist thought, is irrelevant, since he started from that practical human activity that, as Marx said, must be the substance of any intellectual activity. His historical period was quite different from that of the western socialists, who were at this time members of great parties engaged in parliamentary struggles. However, if he went back to Marx's 1848 position, he had to face the basic problem: how are the conditions created that pave the way for a revolution? Marx had thought to no avail in terms of economic crises. Once this theoretical illusion had been destroyed, what could he substitute? A revolutionary party, specialized in the struggle against political police, could achieve some success among the working class if it prepared them ideologically to act at the right moment. Much more was needed, however, to destroy the great machine of a powerful autocracy. Apparently Lenin never arrived at very clear conclusions about the problem, and did not succeed in developing his party of professional revolutionaries to any great extent. When war broke out in 1914, all the leaders were either in jail or outside Russia. History, however, was reserving for him a unique opportunity: Czarism would be slowly bled throughout a long war and would topple under the attack of an inexperienced and weak bourgeoisie. Thus, the prerevolutionary conditions that were not, to Marx's disappointment, created by the economic crises of Europe, were created in Russia by the Great War. In this way, although he had not foreseen it,[13] Lenin could take advantage of a situation whose revolutionary potential had from the very first escaped western socialists, and that was to become for Germany the great lost opportunity.

Lenin attributed considerable importance to ideological issues and affirmed that there could be no revolution without a revolutionary ideology. He saw in ideology a unifying force able to create in the masses great confidence in their leaders, the bearers of a truth whose validity was beyond question. For this reason, he refused to admit any qualifications to the work of his masters, Marx and Engels. He could, however, interpret them, and this he did with extraordinary boldness. At no point did he allow himself to be tied by formal ideological schemes: When he made the most rapid switch of his life, deciding that it was necessary to move from the bourgeois to the proletariat revolution without any transition—which provoked considerable confusion among all contemporary Marxists both in and outside Russia—he declared categorically that "a Marxist must take into account real life and cannot continue to cling to yesterday's theories." [14] In this way, revolutionary theory was elaborated while the revolution was in progress. The important thing was to carry on the revolution, to "become stronger, to be victorious at the right moment and the right time." [15]

We were thus faced with a doctrine in which revolutionary ideology did not arise directly out of the class struggle, but was elaborated by intellectual minorities and spread among the working class by an organization of professional fighters against the political police, or, in other words, specialists in the manipulation of violence. Completely new issues were created, since the terms of the problem could be totally inverted in favor of the bourgeoisie. If the revolution was the work of professionals, the counter-revolution also could be; if a group of specialists could successfully educate the working class in the socialist ideology, another group, particularly if it had at its command immeasurably greater resources, could equally successfully spread a different ideology in the service of bourgeois interests. In other words: if the rise to power of the working class was not the result of *historical necessity* in the dialectical sense, but was chiefly the work of professionally organized groups whose aim it was to put the working class in power, then possibilities for realizing the socialist ideal became very slight.

It was this conclusion that provided the starting point for the bourgeois ideologists who paved the way for fascism. It was precisely the role of Germany—where Engels had witnessed the exemplary experience of the working class organized into a great party, and had pointed to this as the new route to be followed by socialism—to demonstrate the enormous resources at the disposal of a bourgeoisie that chose to travel along the road of violence. In 1851, in analyzing the reasons for the counter-revolution in Germany, Engels called attention to the enormous importance of the great petit-bourgeois mass of the population: "Humble before all strong governments and inclined to liberalism whenever the grand-bourgeoisie rises to power, this class is seized by abject terror whenever the class beneath it, the proletariat, attempts an independent movement." [16] The situation in 1933 was not very different, from the point of view of social stratification, since the great mass of the German population was still not made up of the grand bourgeoisie or the proletariat. The middle classes had replaced the petit bourgeoisie as the largest section of the population; "abject terror" was as lively as ever, as was so clearly demonstrated by the Nazi leaders.

5

The Dialectic of Capitalist Development

Economic development, being fundamentally a process of incorporating and diffusing new techniques, implies changes of a structural nature in both the systems of production and distribution of income. The way in which these changes take place depends, to a large extent, on the degree of flexibility of the institutional framework within which the economy operates. And this flexibility is dependent on the greater or lesser capacity of the ruling classes to go beyond the natural limitations of their ideological horizons.

In a strict sense, economic development is the expansion of the productive system that supports a given society. This expansion only becomes feasible when a mechanism of self-limitation is imposed by the society on the use of the social product. This self-limitation is the necessary condition for accumulation, or the formation of a new productive capacity. On the other hand, the full utilization of this new productive capacity calls for changes in the way the society uses the social product.

Until the emergence of modern planned economies, in which accumulation is the result of deliberate economic policy, the self-limitation imposed by societies in order to expand their productive capacity was always associated with forms of income distribution characterized by extreme inequality. This regime of concentrated wealth always existed side by side with a system of social classes in which minority groups owned the means of production. Private ownership of the means of production can be understood, from the economic point of view, as an expedient which societies resorted to as a way of limiting their use of the social product, thus clearing the way for accumulation.

However, development does not depend solely on accumulation. It depends equally on the dynamic force generated by societies in the form of an impulse to improve living standards. If the increase of the product, resulting from accumulation, were to remain permanently concentrated in the hands of small ruling groups, the process of capital formation would tend to reach saturation point. It is because an appreciable part of the new product is distributed among the working masses that development can continue. The masses tend to consume everything that comes into their hands, and soon become aware that they are subject to a regime of permanent rationing in the satisfaction of their needs. They realize that the self-limiting mechanism of the society operates in a discriminatory way against the groups that have only their work as a source of income.

Development in capitalist societies, that is to say, those in which private ownership of the means of production is prevalent, is based, therefore, on two major forces: first, the impulse to accumulate, which leads the ruling minority to try to limit consumption by the community and at the same time to increase its own power in this community by appropriating a substantial part of the increased product, and second, the impulse to improve living conditions, which acts on the masses by fully incorporating their activities into the monetary economy and by raising and diversifying their patterns of consumption.

In the early stages of development of industrial capitalism —characterized by the growth and rise of a new ruling class that struggles to entrench its power against the influential ruling groups supported by the pre-capitalist structure—the accumulative impulse is the dominating force. These stages are marked by a completely elastic supply of manpower, owing to the breakup of the former handicraft economy. Real wages do not benefit from increased productivity, but the breakup of the handicraft system opens the way for the absorption of an expanding produce from the capitalist sector. The working masses play a relatively minor role in this stage of development, since the dynamic impulse derives chiefly from the struggle of the new ruling class to broaden the economic basis on which its dominating capacity rests.

In the advanced stages of capitalist development, the dynamic pole tends to shift toward the working class. Institutionalization of inequalities in the distribution of income insures an increased supply of resources for accumulation, the limitations operating more on the capacity for effecting new investments than on savings. However, as the availability of manpower loses its early elasticity, the greater part of the pre-capitalist economy having been absorbed, the working masses come to play a much more important role in the dynamics of the development process. Since the labor supply becomes increasingly dependent on a declining natural growth of the population, and at the same time the number of individual working hours is reduced, the accumulation of capital in developed capitalist countries tends to become twice or three times as great as the increase in the labor force. It would be expected, therefore, that there would be growing pressure for an increased share of the social income on the part of the worker, and that this pressure would in turn lead to a reduction in the rate of accumulation, and hence in the rate of growth. The capitalist class would consequently see its relative importance in society diminish with the increase in the workers' share of the total income, and the decline in the strategic importance of its ownership of the means of production.

The actual accumulative impulse would lead, therefore, in the most advanced stages of capitalist development, to the progressive strengthening of the working-class position in the struggle for distribution of the income. However, this tendency was limited by the fact that technology indirectly provided an increase in the availability of labor. Serving the interests of the capitalist class that financed it, technological research conditioned the development of productive processes so that accumulation could maintain a rate high enough to absorb available savings, and at the same time cancel the effects of the relative scarcity of manpower on the distribution of income.

The development of capitalism at its most advanced stage derives its principle dynamic impulse from the aggressive feelings of the working masses who struggle to increase their share of the social product. This aggression, which threatens the profit rate of the capitalist class, arouses in reaction an interest in technological innovations that tend to reduce the manpower required per unit of product. In themselves, these technological inventions are a factor in the creation of unemployment and act as a depressive force on the economy. However, this force is of a very special type since it produces structural changes in the economy, thereby altering the functions of production and reconditioning the pattern of consumption by means of changes in relevant prices. However, it is the action of the working class, in its attempt to gain an increased share of the produce, that creates the conditions necessary for the advance of technology. In turn, technology permits the maintenance of a high rate of accumulation without the brake of an inelastic labor supply.

The capitalist ruling classes, through their control of technical advances and their supervision of the investment process, maintain their basic positions of authority. However, their use of these instruments of domination is strictly limited. If they ignore these limitations, they can provoke unemployment (by an immoderate use of automation, for instance) on a scale that would give rise to a depression that could profoundly affect their profits. As a result of this need for self-control, the capitalist ruling classes are obliged to accept the growing participation of working-class leaders in economic decisions at the levels of both the individual enterprise and the economy in general.

Modern capitalist democracies are the crowning achievement of the evolution of the forces we have outlined. In these democracies, the most important decision centers are in the hands of the capitalist class controlling the means of production. However, the dynamism of these societies depends, in the final analysis, on the aspirations and aggressiveness of the working masses whose participation in political decisions is, for the most part, indirect. In the economic sphere, the action of the masses constitutes the chief factor in development, the ruling classes organizing themselves in a defensive strategy. During periods of war, reconstruction, or rearmament, the reality may deviate from this model, but it tends to revert to it once predomination of non-economic factors over the accumulative process is over.

In this type of society, self-imposed limitations to the exercise of power tend to be the result of the interaction of these forces. The capitalist class maintains its dominant position through a mechanism that leads the society to limit its consumption (the process of saving) for the benefit of minority groups, this brings it into conflict with the working masses. On the other hand, the latter, as their class consciousness develops and they become aware of their antagonism to the capitalist groups, try to increase their share of the product, opening the way for the structural changes that result from the introduction of new techniques. The existence of class antagonisms is therefore inherent in the growth process of this type of society. To this we owe the spontaneous division of certain centers of decision and the mechanism of self-limitation of the exercise of power. Though it is essentially a society ruled by one class, the fundamental characteristic of capitalist democracy is this self-imposed limitation on the exercise of power. The attempts to make it monolithic or totalitarian in the political sphere, have led either to economic stagnation, or to deviations in the growth process, with external aggression or some other non-economic end acting as the dynamic pole. These deviations have inevitably led to a stalemate in the economic sphere.

In order to exist as a society that bases its development on class antagonism, capitalist democracy requires a certain flexibility in its institutions. It is in the nature of class antagonisms that they cannot be overcome within a rigid political-legal system. Conflicts between individuals can be solved within a system of arbitration established by law, since there is always some public interest above the individual interest, and the accepted arbiter of the public interest is the state. However, the same cannot be said of class conflicts, since it would be difficult to determine the public interest without in some way independently defining the interests of the classes that make up the society. The solution of class conflicts by imposing the will of the capitalist class becomes more and more antisocial as development begins to depend on the dynamism and aggression of the working class. The more the capitalist economy develops, the more the interests of the workers incorporate those of the whole community. The capitalist, therefore, becomes progressively less qualified to interpret the real social interest. Hence, the organized strike has become the fundamental instrument of social intercourse in a capitalist democracy. In effect, even during the most difficult moments of the last World War, the most advanced capitalist democracies appealed repeatedly to the strike mechanism in order to solve problems of social coexistence.

Class antagonisms in capitalist democracies express themselves, on the subjective plane, in an ideological polyvalency: a number of ideologies coexist. That is to say, there are different interpretations of the social interest and various plans for the future of the society. In this way, a kind of cultural dualism is created, which no education system succeeds in eradicating and which functions as a backdrop in these societies. However, the dualism of the standards of value does not preclude an awareness of the common interests that do exist. The affinity of interests comes to the surface particularly when the problem of the development-stagnation dichotomy is considered. In the growing stages, all problems seem easy to solve, and in the stagnant phases, the smallest difficulties seem insuperable. In effect, in the growing stages the ideological horizons broaden and the number of overlapping points of view increases. However, the basic ideological ambivalence is always present as a reflex of class antagonism. To remove it would be to take away from a capitalist society one of the essential factors in its dynamism. As modern development took place in the nation-state, through the formation and defense of national markets, the interests of development found their maximum political expression in nationalism, the only ideology able to encompass antagonistic class interests.

As a result of these numerous ideological positions and the self-imposed limitation of power, capitalist democracies are societies that, as a general rule, provide much room for individual action. Individual liberty can assume advanced forms and furnish ample scope for man's creative activity. However, this very climate of ideological conflict only occasionally directs individual creative endeavor toward social construction. Social evolution takes place in a rather random fashion through successive approximations. It is at the mercy of conflicts that are submitted to various forms of arbitration and of the acts of lawmaking bodies. Or it follows in the wake of social tensions, or is guided by the more or less concealed interests of minority groups.

Since the political evolution of the capitalist democracies requires that, on the one hand, the institutional framework be sufficiently steadfast to provide firmness for a system based on class privilege and, on the other, sufficiently flexible to permit constant structural changes in its economic system, this evolution always expressed itself in complex and uncertain historical processes. In countries such as those of Anglo-Saxon origin, where forms of government representing growingly heterogenous social groups had a precocious development, the institutional framework showed a greater capacity for adapting itself to the complex play of class struggles. In those countries, however, where the Byzantine tradition of the legal code gave a greater rigidity to the institutional framework, or where historical conditions permitted autocratic forms of power to persist, capitalist democracy evolved through repeated periods of institutional tension. More or less abortive attempts to institute representative government alternated with spells of dictatorship by minority groups of the capitalist class and occasional revolutionary outbursts, nearly always of uncertain outcome. However, a constant factor in the political evolution of capitalist democracies was the twofold tendency to expand, and at the same time to reduce, the state's functions. The expansion of the state's function as supplier of services was principally the result of urbanization and the emergence of a mass society with growing organizational problems. Simultaneously, there was a tendency to reduce state interference in the productive process and the distribution of the social income. On the one hand, the tendency to provoke hypertrophy in government as the instrument for state action led to the creation of the modern bureaucratic leviathans; on the other, there was the attitude that economic activities should be controlled by bodies outside the immediate range of direct government influence if limited resources were to be exploited with the maximum possible rationality.

The institutional framework supporting capitalism has roots deep in the whole historical process of modern culture. Thus, the idea that economic relations should be subject to general norms, and that state interference in these norms should be limited, found support in the philosophy of natural law and the inalienability of man's basic rights. The property right, considered "inalienable," and acting as the cornerstone of capitalist social organization, provided the link between the above two conflicting attitudes. We must acknowledge that this link permitted the establishment of the basic belief, transposed from the Greek culture to the European, that citizens owed obedience to the laws and not to the governors, who were themselves subject to the laws. However, we must note that the struggle for civil liberties, which was initially bolstered by the demand for freedom of worship, and given a tremendous impetus at the end of the eighteenth century when it was linked to aspirations for national independence during the American Revolution, provided a haven for capitalism in the nineteenth century, when it was embraced by the "laissez-faire" economic doctrine. Thus, capitalism was allowed shelter, in a system based on class privilege, under the same ideological and institutional banner that belonged to the age-old fight to protect fundamental human rights.

The self-imposed limitation of power that we have singled out as the fundamental trait in the operation of a capitalist democracy, would also not be easy to explain outside the context of the European historical process. In effect, modern representative governments have their roots in the struggle for power among feudal oligarchies. This struggle, which lies at the basis of the formation of modern European national states, was, in almost all cases, resolved by setting up autocratic national governments. However, in special cases, it led to a division of power. In England, for instance, the existence of a parliament from the beginning of the thirteenth century, which represented the nobility and limited the power of the monarch to levy taxes and maintain armies, created the conditions for precocious political development. In spite of the ups and downs of the struggle between the royal power and parliament, a system of representative government existed in England a century before the French Revolution. This did not mean that the people were represented in the government, which was elected by the small segment of the population that enjoyed privileges, chiefly those of property. But there is no doubt that for a part of the population at least, the principle had been established that no government can exist without the sanction of the law and that laws are based on the consent of the governed. The task of the nineteenth century was to broaden the bases of this representation, with the resultant tendency to universalize suffrage which was to lead to the formation of present-day capitalist democracies.

The fragmentation of economic power into rival groups on the one hand, and the conflict of social classes on the other, both inherent factors in capitalist democracies, created favorable conditions for the consolidation of representative government in these democracies. At a more advanced stage of their evolution, when the working class began to play a dynamic role fundamental to development, it became impossible to dispense with a degree of elasticity in the centers of decision. This could only be achieved by a government representing large sections of the population. The advance of universal suffrage, inevitable under the urban conditions created by industrial development, permitted this broadening of the bases of political representation. The ruling classes, however, tried to defend their positions by making the fundamental elements of the institutional framework much more rigid. In this way, "constitutions," which had previously been conceived as safeguards of civil liberties and organization norms of the state, began to incorporate all the privileges of the ruling class. Thus, the advance of universal suffrage was, as a rule, paralleled by the codification of constitutions, the legislative power being substantially restricted at the same time that its democratization was permitted. In United States law, transplanted in a weakened version to Brazil, the capacity to decide whether a legal innovation is "constitutional" is the prerogative of the judicial power, necessarily the power most closely linked to the ruling class, since it is excluded from the mechanism of representation.

The fundamental problem of capitalist democracies that are in the process of integrating the working class into the body politic, is to allow the advance of popular representation without compromising the basic institutional framework that shelters the privileges of the ruling class. The handling of this problem calls for great political ability on the part of the leaders of this class. Not that there would be any risk of a spontaneous abandonment of privileged positions, a phenomenon unknown in history, but because of the tendency to take up rigid positions that could create obstacles to social development.

The broader the basis of a representative government, the more it will be in a position to pick up the social tensions created by obstacles to development and to translate these into political terms. In this way, there is room for debate and for the identification of common denominators that allow the government to gather together forces able to resolve the problem with a minimum of damage to the institutional framework. This is only possible when the most important economic and social groups have achieved a high proportion of representation in the government. If this representation is limited or inadequate, the government's ability to sense social tensions at the right time through its principal political organ, the legislative body, will be somewhat restricted. In this case, an outbreak of the repressed forces can be expected, leading to extra-legal political solutions. In almost all the capitalist democracies, the most important changes in the institutional framework have been effected by extra-legal political processes, that is to say, by revolutionary movements. These movements are, as a rule, the result of cleavage within the ruling class and, in most cases, are a way of precipitating inevitable changes. They thus prevent an aggravation of social tension that could cause profounder movements in the social structure and threaten the position of this class. In this way, in revolutionary movements, forces moving in the direction of removing obstacles to social development are interwoven with forces that attempt to slow down genuine democratic processes, these forces often mutually supporting each other.

Thus, certain social conquests are achieved at the same time that popular representation in government is limited by oblique means. As this reduction of the representativeness of government has consequences on the whole social process, reducing the elasticity of institutions and blocking access to further social conquests, the advance achieved by the revolutionary method is merely apparent.

The alternations between evolution within the institutional framework and extra-legal solutions in the development of capitalist societies is a complex problem that can only be understood within a particular historical context. In the first place, we must bear in mind that the two supreme aspirations of modern man in the political sphere—the civil liberties that protect the citizen against any form of arbitrary power, and representative government founded on popular approval that guarantees these liberties and paves the way for further social conquests—are expressions of a historical process that transcends capitalism. If it is true that the structure of capitalist society, with its fragmentation of the centers of decision, facilitated the consolidation of these aspirations, it is equally true that the rigidity of the institutional framework, frequently leading to extra-legal solutions, is, in many cases, a considerable impediment to the democratization process. We need only compare the evolution of industrial capitalism in England and Germany, countries in which this evolution was extremely vigorous, to realize how independent of actual economic development the advance of civil liberties and representative systems of government can be.

There is some historical evidence that, where a certain experience of representative government existed before the Industrial Revolution or during its early stages, the institutional framework showed greater flexibility, and this allowed economic development to proceed without major disruptions of the political systems. It seems that it was also in these cases that the democratization process made most progress. On the other hand, when industrial capitalism penetrated into societies where representative government was practically unknown, economic development provoked repeated ruptures in the political process, through movements combining revolutionary and counter-revolutionary elements. In this case, the progress of the democratization process, that is to say, the realization of the basic political aspirations previously referred to, was much more limited.

Even under the most favorable historical conditions, however, a capitalist regime does not necessarily lead to the attainment of economic development together with progressive democratization of the bases of political power. The reasons are bound up with the particular inner dynamic of the system. In effect, at the most advanced stage of capitalism, the economic process calls for progressive action on the part of the central decision-making agents, as a requisite for the maintenance of stability in conditions of development. In this way, the old "laissez-faire" economies tended to be replaced by "mixed" economies, in which the state directly controls important sectors of production, orients technology, and indirectly conditions investment by the private sector. Thus, to the tendency, previously noted, toward the growth of the state-machine as supplier of services, is added this second tendency, directly linked to the economic process.

The unprecedented growth of the state-machine in capitalist societies, which occurred chiefly after the First World War, took place at a time when the control of government was, in most cases, in the hands of a small ruling class united around a cluster of privileges. The democratization of the bases of political power, then in its early stages, began to encounter a new kind of obstacle. This was the increasing expansion of the state-machine that extended the influence of the administration, transforming it into a new power able to condition the behavior of political organs in important sectors. Since this bureaucratic machine, with its profound ramifications in the economic system, had been established by a government controlled by a small ruling class, it came to represent a powerful factor in the defense of the status quo. Thus, the political effectiveness of the representative system of government was reduced even before the bases of political power had been fully democratized by increased representation in government. In short, the phase of democratization, characterizing a period of predominating representative organs in government, gave way to a phase of mass organization, marking a period in which political controversy is restricted to secondary issues, and fundamental decisions are made at the administrative level.

The more advanced stage of bureaucratization of capitalist democracies does not necessarily represent a setback for basic political advantages already gained. The administrative power is essentially conservative, since it is subject to impersonal and more or less unchanging norms. This inertia contains a certain element of self-restraint that renders it difficult to make incursions of an arbitrary nature, even by those in power. Advantages gained by citizens find a certain measure of protection in the administrative power. But the subtle way in which expansion of the administrative agencies takes place favors the preservation of representative bodies with all their ritual, and these bodies then adapt themselves to the new realities of the exercise of power. Complete mass organization and bureaucratization of a capitalist society would signify the final incorporation of the privilege system, defended by the ruling class, into the social structure. These privileges would then come to be considered as one of the *a priori* elements of an incontestable social value scale.

The basic problem is therefore how to prevent frustration of the process of effective democratization caused by a too-early extension of bureaucratization and mass organization? In other words, how can government be given fully effective representativeness before the class in power has had the opportunity to protect its constellation of privileges by erecting the insurmountable wall of administrative power and reducing the political process to a mere formal game? A positive solution for this problem would seem to require an acceleration of the political process incompatible with the degree of flexibility of the institutional framework in a capitalist regime. Yet, a revolutionary outlet has inevitably led to political regression. In a class society characterized by ideological ambivalence, this problem must, by definition, remain unresolved. The clash of these irreducible positions will create the historical conditions that will determine the most workable solution.

Present-day underdeveloped structures constitute a special case within capitalist evolution. The economy that antedated the industrialization process was, in this case, of a colonial type, which signifies domination by ruling groups subject to a Ptolemaic alienation, i.e., to a structural incapacity to understand their own positions in the play of forces. On the other hand, the technological innovations absorbed by these economies are not the outcome of internal economic evolution but are "borrowings" from much more advanced systems. As industrialization is chiefly oriented toward substitution for imports, technological transplantation takes place in terms of the price structure of the importing sector and not in terms of the economy as a whole. Therefore, investment can lead to the creation of unemployment in spite of the existence of large, underemployed masses both within the monetary economy and outside it. This explains why the economies of present-day underdeveloped structures are not very dynamic and have strong internal tendencies toward stagnation. Conditions that tend to convert the working masses into a dynamic factor only very gradually emerge. As in the case of technological assimilation, organization of the workers reflects sectorial criteria, and not those of the productive forces as a whole. The struggle for an increased share of the product is not led by the workers as a body, but by minority groups who occupy strategic positions. Consequently, it becomes possible for the capitalist class to divert pressure to the mass of consumers so that the workers themselves pay for the increased wages of the privileged labor minorities, and the capitalist class incurs no losses in its share of the product. Since the growth of these economies is basically dependent on the activities of the groups responsible for the accumulative process, the historical conditions under which these groups emerged, and those under which they operate, must be considered in each specific case, if we are to distinguish the possibilities for growth in a particular society with an underdeveloped economic structure within the capitalist dynamic.

6

Political Consequences of Underdevelopment

Underdevelopment must be initially understood in terms of the social structure. The fact that the better studied and better known aspects of underdevelopment are the economic ones, is a simple confirmation of the general theory that the dominant role in the process of social development is generally played by economic factors. The characterization of underdevelopment in purely economic terms, being a much simpler task, is a perfectly legitimate initial formulation of the problem. It would be completely wrong, however, to expect that economists, using the analytical methods at their disposal, could exhaust a subject which involves important aspects that can only be approached by sociologists or political scientists. Consideration of underdevelopment in terms of income per capita is, however, one of the obsessions of our time and creates a serious handicap for understanding the problem on the historical plane. It was the economists who undertook the difficult task of pioneering in the field of social research, but it is no longer possible to continue simply to use their work as a basis for studying this complex subject. We still speak of economic planning as if it were a question of choice among techniques elaborated by able economists, when in fact planning presupposes the formulation of policy, and specific attitudes toward the rationality aimed at in political economy. It is obvious that politics cannot be considered except in terms of the factors conditioning the exercise of power, and this involves going beyond "analytical models" to consider "practical human activity" within a given historical reality.

In underdeveloped social structures, by virtue of the simple fact that the inelastic supply of productive factors (particularly the land) is of relatively major importance, division of social work and private appropriation of the means of production is reflected in the marked differentiation of classes. In effect, most of the underdeveloped countries are basically agricultural; the bulk of the population is made up of peasants opposed to a minority of landowners and merchants. However, this clear social differentiation has contributed nothing to the formation of class consciousness. As Engels had already noted: "The agricultural populace, in view of the fact that it is spread over a wide area, and that it experiences difficulty in finding the basis for understanding, never initiates an independence movement." [1] The reason for the weakness of class-consciousness among the peasants is simple: in an agricultural economy, particularly where feudal or semi-feudal forms still predominate, antagonism of class interests does not play a dominant role. Since the harvest depends on weather conditions, the responsibility for "good years" and "bad years" is credited to nature. Where paid agricultural work is introduced, it seems progressive, since it nearly always represents a rise in real wages and affects only a fraction of the agricultural population. The urban artisan who became proletarianized felt that he was going down in the social scale, but the small rural sharecropper who manages to get paid work imagines that he has gone up.

The relative importance of the land as a productive factor and the "social peace" that traditionally reigned in the country areas, in contrast to the atmosphere of the cities, always gave the landowning class tremendous political ascendency in underdeveloped countries. Under these conditions, the state tends to acquire a large number of the characteristics of an instrument for domination by one class. Nevertheless, it would be wrong to see in it the "repressive force" to which Engels so often referred. For the state to become a repressive force (and in many cases this does happen), the class struggle must first have assumed great importance in the society. This is not the case in underdeveloped countries, particularly in the agricultural sector, which is the principal base of political power in these societies.

What we have regarded as underdevelopment is less the existence of a basically agricultural economy—in this case we would merely be dealing with a *backward* economy—than the occurrence of a structural dualism. This originates when, owing to certain historical conditions, a wedge of typically capitalist economy is introduced into a "backward" agricultural economy, creating an inbalance at the factors level (to use the economic jargon) with repercussions throughout the social structure. The conditions created by this structural dualism cannot easily be explained in terms of a stable equilibrium model. The dynamic scheme of cumulative causation, elaborated by Myrdal, is much more effective in explaining this case. Given the existence of two forms of remuneration for work, two technologies at extremely different levels, two concepts of organization of production, a dual economy is intrinsically unstable.

If we consider the social structure of an underdeveloped system as a whole, we can distinguish two factors that could provide a dynamic impulse: the internal conflicts of the capitalist sector, and the tensions created between this sector and the pre-existing economy. There are important aspects of these interrelations that give a specific nature to the developmental process in a dual structure. Thus, development of the capitalist sector is achieved mainly by absorbing factors from the former economy, or, whenever it suits the capitalists, by absorbing new techniques. This possibility of alternative solutions gives the capitalist class particular advantages over the industrial workers. In effect, the existence of a large reserve of manpower at the disposal of the capitalists is a factor that inhibits the whole process of class struggle. In this way, the capitalist sector in underdeveloped economies is, as a rule, not very dynamic. The ruling class becomes accustomed to a high rate of profit that is never effectively challenged by the class struggle. This is why, in many underdeveloped economies, the capitalist sector remains practically at a standstill, achieving the same social peace that characterized the old feudal structure, synonymous with stagnation and once described as "the peace of the tomb." A good example of this situation was the Northeastern textile industry in Brazil, created towards the end of the last century, which was exactly like the sugar industry in the paternalistic methods it employed.

We do not intend, at this point, to raise the problem of the growth of an underdeveloped economy directly, but it must be remembered that in the early stages of this growth, a fundamental role is played by exogenous factors, through the activities of the exporting sector. The impulse given by this sector for growth is decisive for the development of the capitalist "wedge," both with regard to activities related to export and those related to the domestic market. What needs to be stressed is the reduced internal dynamism of a dual economy, deriving from characteristics peculiar to its capitalist sector. However, the relations of this sector to the existing agricultural economy go much further than the simple transfer of manpower. The increased demand for agricultural products in the urban areas, generated by development of the capitalist sector, necessarily has strong effects on the rural sector, already subject to a constant drain in manpower. In this way, the pressure tends to divide the rural sector by causing it to submit part of its activities to the direct control of capitalist entrepreneurs. Consequently, an unstable situation is created for the former landowning class, which attempts to find support for the protection of its privileges in political institutions. As the stability of the old social structure is reduced, the struggle for power gains in importance, and, as a rule, it then becomes an important new factor in this very instability.

The ruling class in an underdeveloped country tends to be divided into three main groups: the original nucleus of landowners, the group controlling interests connected with external trade (always with wide foreign links) and the capitalists basically supported by the internal market. The first group is, generally, in favor of free trade and has an anti-state bias, i.e., it is opposed to any change in the status quo, which it thinks would have to come through state action. The second group also favors free trade but its liberalism is already qualified, since it soon learns to use the state-machine in order to defend its external trade. The third group is protectionist, and in many ways has a pro-state bias, attempting to use the state-machine through credit, exchange, control, and other means, in order to transfer resources for its own benefit. The discrepancies between these groups are not very different from those that could have been observed in Europe at the time industrial capitalism was implanted, between the rural aristocracy, the financial "grand bourgeoisie," and the industrial bourgeoisie. However, whereas in nineteenth-century Europe, genuine class struggle between wage earners and capitalists grew in importance and conditioned the whole social process, in underdeveloped structures this does not occur. In the absence of a genuine challenge within the underdeveloped structure itself, the dominant groups remain unable to solve their internal contradictions, and this affects social development in an adverse way. Thus, the landowning group that controls a large part of the political power through its rural "basis," and acts as a depressive force on the developmental process, can maintain its dominating influence for a considerable length of time. In the same way, foreign interests linked to the exporting sector, can, for the benefit of this sector, hinder the growth of an internal market without provoking reactions of any great consequence within the economic system itself. Hence the notorious tendency to stagnate that characterizes many present-day underdeveloped economies, has roots deep in their social structures.

We must call attention to one final point in the characterization of underdeveloped economies. This is the extraordinary importance that the state tends to assume in these structures. In addition to the numerous causes of the growth of the state-machine in modern times, regardless of the degree of development, the internal instability of the ruling class involves an increase in the value attributed to positions of power. Domestic capitalism, faced with the free trade bias of the exporting and agricultural sectors in general, requires strong state protection in order to survive. The agricultural sector, under pressure from the capitalist group, needs credit support on a large scale in order to progress, and only the state is in a position to offer this. The exporting sector needs an underlying structure of basic services in order to establish itself, and this calls for decisive participation by the state. This rapid expansion of the state-machine, coupled with an increase in the provision of general services in the urban areas (to a large extent a consequence of the concentration of income), is reflected in a vigorous expansion of the salaried middle class, concentrated in the urban areas, with effects of no small importance in the political sphere.

In short, the social structure corresponding to a dual economy can be outlined as follows: at the top is the ruling class composed of various groups of interests, in many respects antagonistic to each other, therefore unable to formulate a plan for national developments, and holding the monopoly of power unchallenged; lower down we have a great mass of salaried urban workers employed in services, which forms a social strata rather than a proper class; beneath this is the class of industrial workers, which hardly represents one-tenth of the active population of the country but constitutes its most homogeneous sector; and finally, the peasant masses, whose characteristics have already been defined. Because of the absence of genuine class struggle characterizing a capitalist economy, the development of class-consciousness among the workers tends to be an extremely slow process. It is precisely through the growth of a class-consciousness that working-class ideology is formed, although this process can be strongly influenced by the historical experience of other countries and the interpretation of intellectuals. In many underdeveloped countries—and Brazil is a good example—a prolonged inflationary process helps to distort the original characteristics of the class struggle. In effect, in an inflationary situation, wage increases interest the employers as much as the employees, since it is clear that the consumer is the one who has to pay in the end. The point at which the consumer will pay or not is a decision that rests in the hands of the state, whose power is thus enormously increased. Therefore, it is much more important to control the instruments of political power than to struggle against strikers, since it is through these instruments that the decision is made as to who will finally foot the bill.

In an underdeveloped country with the characteristics we have described, the political process tends to take the form of a constant struggle for power among the groups that make up the ruling class, because of the extraordinary importance of the control of the state-machine. Since there is no endogenous process in the system capable of stimulating the growth of class-consciousness among the industrial working masses, the latter remain as liable as the salaried middle-class workers to be manipulated by ruling-class ideologies designed to serve the conflicting inner factions. These ideologies, known under the generic form of populism, use the common language of what in the nineteenth century was called "Utopian Socialism," the essence of which is the promise of some sort of redistribution of the social product, without considering the organization of production. The danger of populism is that it succeeds in redistributing income for the benefit of certain groups and to the detriment of others, even if this is only for a limited period of time. In this way, it becomes a powerful weapon in the hands of one faction of the ruling class against the others. In an inflationary period, when credit becomes enormously important, this weapon can be used with considerable effect. In populist politics, the people—the salary- and wage-earning classes and small income groups—are invariably manipulated to frighten the enemy and permit the take-over of key positions. However, temporary victories are won at the cost of favors granted to certain groups and promised to others. Inflation, which allows favors to be dispensed with one hand and taken away with the other, opens enormous possibilities for populist action. The most serious consequence of populism, from the point of view of social development, is that it misleads the workers and prevents them from realizing their own interests. As Lenin said: "Demagogues are the worst enemies of the working class. The worst, precisely, because they arouse the bad instincts of the masses, since it is impossible for unprepared workers to recognize their enemies, who present themselves, sometimes sincerely, as their friends." [2]

Under certain conditions, the populist game can become extremely dangerous for the ruling class itself, with the workers increasing their claims, or demanding the fulfillment of promises made at the height of electioneering enthusiasm. These circumstances favor take-overs by bold leaders of minority groups within the ruling class itself. In this way emerge the familiar dictatorships of underdeveloped countries, whose chief end is to give greater stability to the social structure and to consolidate the position of the ruling class under the dominance of one of its factions. Once the internal quarrels of the ruling class have been reduced, the importance of the populace as a "maneuvering reserve" is likewise reduced. In order to strengthen his position, the dictator may consider it more effective to promote his personal prestige among the masses by means of intense propaganda, making slight concessions so that they may be exaggerated. From the point of view of social development, these periods of "strong government" have extremely negative effects. The working class ceases to gain its own achievements and small concessions are granted from above, regardless of the needs of society as a whole. On the other hand, the increased rigidity of the social structure reduces the possibility that the social conflict endogenous to a capitalist economy will have a chance to exercise its renovating action, and this has negative repercussions on development. There have been cases in which the dictator has been unable to gain the support he needed from the ruling class in order to consolidate his position. In this case, although far from desiring change in the social structure, he will have to graft populist techniques onto the dictatorial regime, using the populace as a maneuvering reserve for exerting pressure on the recalcitrant ruling groups. Of all the forms of populism, this is socially the most pernicious, since, while it prevents the working class from organizing itself around its own program, it involves the workers in a fictitious class struggle that can be taken no more seriously than a Roman circus.

In underdeveloped countries, all "strong governments" created by coups d'état tend to be necessarily right-wing, even though to begin with quite different aims may have been present in the minds of some of its authors. Because it was established as the result of a coup, this type of government must make use of the existing machine to achieve any degree of immediate effectiveness. And without this, it will wither away, or, in other words, it will lose the support of the public opinion required to maintain a minimum of legitimacy, without which it cannot survive. Now, the most viable short-term actions are precisely those that can be undertaken using the methods already established and the instruments already available. In fact, governments that come to power through extra-legal methods, even if they call themselves "strong," are at first extremely weak and gain strength in proportion as they come to terms with established interests and the organized groups that still retain some power. At first these pacts are made to gain time, but finally they are entered into because the initial objectives have been forgotten and only the desire to stay in power remains.

The attainment or maintenance of an open democratic regime in which the wage earners can organize themselves to fight for their own objectives, must be considered as a necessary condition for social development in an underdeveloped country. It is from this point that we can start thinking in terms of political action for development, since populism can only be overcome by movements that have developed within the working class, movements that can lead to the worker's political self-determination.

If it is fundamental to maintain an open democratic regime in which urban wage earners can find a place, it is no less fundamental to extend this political regime to the great mass of peasants. In the majority of underdeveloped countries, including Brazil, so-called democratic society is practically closed to participation by the peasant mass. Excluded from voting by a compulsory illiteracy, this immense mass has almost no voice in the political life of the country. It was about political action in a similarly closed society that Lenin so rightly said: "This struggle must be organized *according to all the rules of art* by professionals of revolutionary action." [3]

Fortunately for the Brazilian revolutionary process, the peasant mass is not isolated; it can count on the effective support of urban organizations, thus increasing its strength for action that will be more effective than the simple use of violence. However, while current political discrimination against the peasant mass continues to exist, it is only to be expected that in more than one case, Leninist-type revolutionary techniques will be used, and in certain cases, will prove truly effective. The movement of the Peasant Leagues is a good example of political action organized along revolutionary lines that proved extremely effective in obtaining objectives later encompassed within the "legal" framework. The organization of the masses for acting within the interplay of the class struggle is based on objectives that can be defined in rational terms; i.e., they appear to the worker as viable in terms of the means being mobilized. The same cannot be said of the organization of a mass excluded from any political activity. In this case, it may be necessary to appeal to a Sorelian type of myth, and Julião [4] must have had some reason to speak to the peasants of "guerilla warfare" and a "new Sierra Maestra." These myths must have seemed to them much more real and much more viable than the wage increase they later managed to gain.

The political objective to keep in sight in underdeveloped countries—the objective that will assure the most rapid economic development in a pluralist democratic society—is the creation of conditions under which both urban wage earners and the peasant mass will be given effective participation in the formation of power. The present ruling class in Brazil represents only a fragment of the politically active population. In the past, this fragment could be taken for the nation as a whole, since it was made up of the small minority of the population for whom political activity had any meaning, or whose activities could have any relevant effects on the destiny of the country. Today, the activities of the working masses, both urban and rural, are of fundamental importance to the economic and social development of the country. This means that such activities must be incorporated into the political process. Such broadening of the political bases is essential, if the process of social change that has already started is to proceed with a minimum of cost to the community. There is no doubt that a period of social revolution has opened for Brazil. It remains to be seen whether this revolutionary process will develop as "practical critical activity" or as the tragedy of a people who failed to find their destiny.

PART TWO

Diagnosis of the Brazilian Crisis

7

The Brazilian Economy: A Broad Survey

Present Stage of Development

Brazil, as an economic and cultural expression, is surely one of the least known countries outside its own frontiers. And even less known are the profound changes that have occurred in the last quarter of a century, during which period an essentially rural nation, made up of great estates specializing in the production of a few tropical commodities, has changed to a semi-industrial economy with considerable masses of its population concentrated in urban areas.

As a geographical expression, Brazil, with its 3,288,000 square miles, is among the five largest countries in the world. No other country in the tropical region is of comparable size. Brazil's population places it among the eight nations having the greatest demographic expression. Its population, which in 1964 was close to 80 million inhabitants, is growing at an annual rate of 3.2 percent, the highest rate among the heavily populated nations. In the western world, only the United States now has a greater population than Brazil. The Brazilian urban population is at present 35 million and is growing at a rate much higher than that of the country as a whole.

What is the present relative importance, in an economic sense, of Brazil? Its Gross Internal Product, measured in dollars with a purchasing power comparable to that of the United States, is close to 30 billion dollars,[1] which places it eleventh among the present-day nations of the world. Of the group of eight nations with the highest population figures, only the United States, the USSR, and Japan have a higher per capita income than Brazil; China, India, Pakistan, and Indonesia have a lower income.

If we accept per capita income as the chief indication of a country's degree of development, Brazil must be classified as a typical underdeveloped country. However, in the world context—with an average income per head estimated at about $380 for 1962—Brazil is in an intermediary position, or at least is at the highest level of the group of underdeveloped countries. From the statistics available on the per capita income of all nations, we can make the comparison shown in table 1.[2]

TABLE 1
RATIOS OF PER CAPITA INCOME

Brazil	100
Countries with free-enterprise economies	
Developed	460
Underdeveloped	60
Socialist countries	
Developed	230
Underdeveloped	45

The level of per capita income coupled with the size of the population provides Brazil with a sufficiently large domestic market to permit some autonomous industrial development. In effect, the principal characteristic of postwar Brazilian development has been the constant substitution of locally manufactured products for previously imported manufactures, with a steady decline in the total amount of imported goods available for the domestic market. The relative importance of national industry in supplying the domestic market can be gauged from the fact that the population spent only 0.1 percent of the income available for consumption on durable imported consumer goods in 1959–1960, and 0.5 percent of this income on non-durable imported goods.[3] In this same period, imports of manufactured consumer goods did not exceed 6.4 percent of the total value of Brazilian imports. A similar degree of substitution of domestic goods has been achieved in construction materials, since the participation of this type of import in the total inversion has been reduced to 1.4 percent for the same period.[4] Table 2 shows the degree

TABLE 2
PRODUCTION AND CONSUMPTION OF INTERMEDIATE GOODS IN BRAZIL IN 1961

	Production	*Apparent Consumption*
	(thousand metric tons)	
Steel	2500	3000
Aluminium	19	42
Lead	13	30
Copper	2	39
Zinc	2	41
Caustic Soda	78	187
Sodium carbonate	44	105
Wood pulp	300	380
Newsprint	62	211
Cement	4711	4709
Gasoline	4800	15000
Coal	2390	3150
Fertilizers		
Nitrogen	12	55
Phosphate	70	119
Potassium	—	71

of Brazilian industrial development in the production of the principal intermediary goods in 1961.

Brazilian industry has also developed appreciably in the production of equipment in general. The output of vehicles, automobiles, and trucks reached 192,000 units in 1962, and the output of tractors for the same period was 7,500 units. Domestic production accounted for a sizable part of the total supply of industrial equipment in 1962. Participation in total supply is high, even in the specialized sectors such as heavy electrical equipment and operating machinery in general.

In short, the degree of industrial development achieved by Brazil makes it possible for the country's demand for consumer goods to be met almost entirely by domestically produced goods, and allows investment based chiefly on the internal supply of capital goods. Imports continue to play their fundamental role as instruments for transmitting the most advanced technology available in the more highly developed centers. However, the country's level of domestic activity is no longer chiefly dependent on the quantity and prices of the products exported. The experience of recent years has shown that, even during a period when exports decline, investment oriented toward the domestic market can be maintained at an adequate level, assuring a high rate of growth.

Physical Background

The vast territory of Brazil, extending approximately 2,600 miles from north to south and covering an equal area from east to west, can be divided into five zones for the purposes of a brief description of the country's economy: the humid coastal belt, the semi-arid Northeast hinterland, the central plateau, the southern pampas, and the Amazon basin.

The humid coastal strip extends along almost the entire east coast, from the State of Rio Grande Do Norte in the north, to the State of Paraná in the south. On the whole, it is a narrow strip, only occasionally exceeding 60 miles in width. The climate is hot and humid. It was on this narrow strip of land, in the Northeastern segment, that the Portuguese started cultivating sugarcane at the beginning of the sixteenth century, thus laying the economic foundations for the territorial occupation of Brazil.

A few dozen kilometers from the Northeast coast, there is a sudden change of climate, the precipitation dropping from

2,000 millimeters to less than 1,000, and in some parts falling to less than 500 millimeters. This is an extensive crystalline plateau with an altitude ranging between 200 and 1,000 meters. Although the precipitation is relatively high, evaporation is always 2 to 4 times greater than the precipitation, and the retention of subterranean water is very limited. The semiaridity of the climate is aggravated by periodic droughts that sometimes last as long as two or three years. In this region, stock-raising was developed from the sixteenth century onward, and was linked to the sugar economy of the coastal zone. The cattle were at first destined to supply traction animals for the sugar mills, but as time went on, they were also used to produce hides for export.

The moist coastal belt becomes narrower around the States of Rio de Janeiro and São Paulo, with a sudden transition to the plateau, which generally loses altitude as it advances eastward and northward into the interior. In contrast to the Northeast hinterland, this region of the Brazilian interior has abundant and regular rainfall, and the soils are of a superior quality. In the northern, mountainous part of this region (the State of Minas Gerais), gold was exploited from the beginning of the eighteenth century, succeeding sugar as the second dynamic factor in the territorial occupation of Brazil. In the colonial period the gold economy attracted an important contingent of European settlers, reducing the relative importance of the African component which had hitherto been the most numerous. In the southern part of this region, beginning in the States of Rio de Janeiro and Minas Gerais and spreading toward São Paulo, the coffee economy developed in the middle of the nineteenth century, dominating the whole process of the Brazilian economy until the third decade of this century. The development of the coffee economy also attracted an important contingent of European immigrants, estimated at more than two million, who settled primarily in the State of São Paulo.

The central plateau slopes gradually as it enters the State

of Rio Grande do Sul and gives way to an extensive plain that enjoys a temperate climate. This region was populated by the Portuguese from the seventeenth century onward, with the aim of fixing the frontier that had remained fluid until after independence. In the eighteenth century, with the development of the mineral industry in the country's central region, a great market for traction animals grew up, and this permitted the southern region—which furnished exceptional conditions for cattle-raising—to develop commercially feasible production, and to link up with the other regions of the country, finally becoming integrated into the Brazilian economy.

The Amazon basin occupies more than half of the Brazilian territory and is almost entirely covered with equatorial forests. Penetration of this immense region began in the seventeenth century by the Jesuits, who managed to create an extensive net of native colonies specializing in the collection of forest products. The Portuguese took over from the Jesuits in the eighteenth century, without, however, succeeding in keeping up the rudimentary economic system that had been established in the Jesuit colonies. Toward the end of the nineteenth century, with the development of rubber extraction, the demand for which had increased at a fantastic rate with the growth of the automobile industry, there was an important influx of immigrants to Amazonia, drawn almost exclusively from the Northeast. However, this vast region still harbors less than 4 percent of the population.

Historical Background

Brazil was the first region in the western hemisphere to develop on an agricultural basis. In a period when only the mining of precious metals justified the colonization of American territories, the Portuguese started an export agriculture along the moist coastal strip of Brazil. Having developed sugar production in their Atlantic islands before the discovery of America, the Portuguese evolved a technique of tropical agriculture that gave them a tremendous advantage over the other European nations that participated in the colonization of the New World. During the sixteenth and first half of the seventeenth centuries, Brazil held virtually a monopoly on the exportation of sugar, then the chief agricultural product in international trade, at a stage when the European market for this product was rapidly expanding. In the 1620's, as a result of Portugal's annexation by Spain, and the war between Spain and the Netherlands, the Brazilian sugar region was invaded by the Dutch, who controlled the sugar refineries and commercial distribution in Europe. After having occupied the Northeast for a quarter of a century, the Dutch were expelled from the region, but since they had mastered the techniques of sugar production, they set up a rival economy in the Antilles, thus putting an end to the Brazilian monopoly. This was the beginning of a long period of decline for the country, interrupted in the first decade of the eighteenth century by the discovery of gold in the central region.

During the eighteenth century, Brazilian economy was dominated by the production of gold and diamonds. Brazil became the chief source of gold for the European economy during the important transformations that immediately preceded the Industrial Revolution. The development of the southern region, including Rio de Janeiro, began during this period. Not only did the population of this region overtake that of the Northeast in number, but the European settlers overtook those of African origin, owing to the predominance of gold over sugar production.

Gold and diamond production declined abruptly during the last decades of the eighteenth century. However, the disturbances in the world market that started with the American Revolution and continued with the French Revolution and Napoleonic Wars, offered new prospects for Brazilian agricultural exports. This new period of agricultural development was only consolidated, however, toward the middle of the nineteenth century, when coffee began to emerge as a great new export product. It was coffee that caused, in the last quarter of the nineteenth century, the most important current of European migration to Brazil and permitted the São Paulo region to become the most densely populated region in the country. After the first decade of the present century, the coffee economy showed all the symptoms of crisis, facing successive periods of overproduction, and requiring government intervention in the market to hold back large quantities of the crop. These crises culminated in 1930 when wide scale destruction of surplus stocks of coffee began.

If we consider the four centuries between 1530—the beginning of the economic occupation of the territory—and 1930, we will see that throughout this entire period the Brazilian economy derived its dynamic impulse from external demands. Three long cycles characterize the development of the country: the first, dominated by sugar exportation (1530–1650); the second, by gold extraction (1700–1780); and the third, by the expansion of the coffee economy (1840–1930). The two intermediate periods, relatively stagnant economically, were distinguished by internal tensions and political events of great significance. During the first (1650–1700), the great movement of territorial expansion took place, which extended Brazilian territory far beyond the limits originally envisaged in the agreement with Spain. The second period was marked by the political separation from Portugal, and the struggles that consolidated the monarchical and unitarian form of government which proved strong enough to keep the vast territory united as one national state.

Economic development, during this long period, consisted essentially of the occupation of new lands or the exploitation of exhaustible natural resources on the one hand, and of the importation of manpower from Africa and Europe on the other. One area was developed while others, whose natural resources had been exhausted or whose exportable products were no longer in demand, remained stagnant or began to decline. As the development of one area had little or no influence on the others, the regions that had declined at earlier periods survived by supporting themselves on subsistence forms of economy, with no inner impulse for growth. This explains the lack of continuity in Brazilian development and the enormous disparity of material living standards in the different regions.

The phase of development based on extensive use of natural resources to satisfy an external demand came to an end with the 1929 crisis. The depression of the 'thirties, by halving the external capacity to pay over a considerable period, led to the beginning of a great productive effort, directed toward the needs of the home market. The transition was in certain ways facilitated by the government's policy of supporting the coffee growers during the prolonged depression. Since coffee culture is perennial, the government decided to guarantee minimum prices for the growers, in order to avoid an even greater crisis, and bought up the large surplus production, even though it was then compelled to destroy a large part of it.

The enormous effort involved in the destruction of surplus coffee had the effect of a bold compensatory policy, and kept up the level of internal demand. Although it created an inflationary pressure that has continued right up to the present, the policy of expanding monetary income created favorable characteristics in the domestic market at a time when the overseas markets were in the throes of the great depression. Thus, for the first time, there was the beginning of a period of development based on internal demand which expressed itself, as a rule, in the form of an attempt to substitute domestic articles for imported manufactured ones.

The development of Brazil after the 'thirties was fundamentally based on industrialization. Investment, which had hitherto been directed toward the expansion of coffee and other export articles, was now turned toward the manufacturing industry with the aim of meeting the internal demand, previously satisfied by imports. This investment had two significant effects: on the one hand, it created the conditions in which the demand itself could grow; on the other, it led to a reduction of the capacity to import the goods previously acquired abroad, since a new demand was created for the import of raw materials, intermediary products, and equipment. In this way, the policy of industrialization, oriented toward a replacement of imported goods, in itself created the need for imports. In proportion as the replacement policy advanced, the industries that had to be established became increasingly heavily capitalized, which in turn created the need to import increased quantities of equipment. This is why pressure on the import capacity remained heavy throughout the period when an effort was being made to replace imports. This constant pressure on the external sector created a serious handicap for the Brazilian economy, whose tendency to raise the level of prices and to incur foreign debts is all too well-known.

Potential Resources

The true possibilities for the future development of a country the size of Brazil could only be appreciated if there were a much more detailed knowledge of its natural resources than is at present available. Lack of knowledge about these resources is itself, however, one of the characteristics of underdevelopment. In the case of Brazil, this difficulty is aggravated by the peculiar characteristics of the country itself. Currently available technology, which has been developed almost exclusively in areas with temperate climatic conditions, often proves to have serious limitations when applied to tropical regions, such as those that make up so much of the vast Brazilian territory. Thus, the immense forest resources of Brazil, concentrated in the Amazon basin, are awaiting improvements of the still primitive technology for exploiting heterogeneous forests. The same applies to the cultivation of the soil. Extensive areas of Brazilian territory, where the rainfall is good and the soils have favorable physical characteristics, are not utilized for lack of adequate agricultural techniques, even when they are close to urban centers. Thus, in the Northeast, where population pressure is already beginning to make itself felt, despite proximity to the coast and available transport facilities, there are three million unused hectares [5] of plainlands awaiting technological development that will permit chemical correction of the soil under economically feasible conditions. The same can be said of the lands known as "cerrados" (closed pasture lands), located in the central part of the country.

Having made these qualifications, we can affirm that the basis of natural resources in Brazil is sufficient for the country's development, over the next decades, to proceed without any major difficulties. Preliminary soil studies have led to the delimitation of an arable area covering about 53 million hectares, that is, practically double the area presently under cultivation.[6] Of these lands, only a fraction requires irrigation. On the other hand, the average yield of the land presently under cultivation can be greatly increased, using techniques already tested in Brazil. It is this abundance of arable land that makes it possible for agricultural development to continue on an extensive scale. Thus, between 1952 and 1961, the 57 percent quantum increase in agricultural production was more than four-fifths, owing to an increase of the land area cultivated, and less than one-fifth of this increase was caused by an improved yield per acre. In this way, the development of Brazilian agriculture continues to take place in the form of simply shifting the frontier. This was the case with coffee cultivation in the 'fifties in the northern Paraná, and it is happening now with the rice fields of east Maranhão.

Water resources are abundant practically throughout the territory, no region being actually desert or arid. Economically feasible hydroelectric potential has been estimated at 30 million kilowatts.[7] Less than one-sixth of this potential is at present being utilized.

Studies of the reserves of mineral resources, although incomplete, illustrate the country's potentialities. Brazil has exceptionally important reserves of iron ore. The known reserves have been estimated at 9,254 million metric tons, and the suspected reserves total 7,000 million, with an ore content of 60 percent, which represents two-thirds of the total Latin American reserves and 20 percent of the world's reserves.[8] The relative importance of potential reserves is still greater. Manganese reserves are 60 million metric tons, with an average ore content of 38–50 percent, representing two-thirds of the Latin American reserves. Proven reserves of bauxite indicate that there are 173 million metric tons of potential mineral. Nickel, tin, and zinc reserves are equally large. However, the copper and lead reserves discovered up to now are of relatively secondary importance.

With respect to fossil fuel resources, Brazil is at present in a far less favorable position. Known reserves of coal are relatively large (1,700 million tons), but the coal is of poor quality. Petroleum reserves, discovered a few years ago, are growing rapidly, but are still relatively small.

Postwar Development

The postwar period has been characterized by rapid growth and important changes in the economic structure. Between 1947 and 1961, the average annual rate of growth was 5.8 percent, equivalent in per capita terms to about 3.0 percent. In the second half of this period there was a distinct rise in the rate of growth, which went up to 7.0 percent between 1957 and 1961, corresponding to a per capita rate of growth of 3.9 percent. Thus, despite the more rapid population growth, the rate of development had increased. Table 3 shows the rates of growth of the gross product and the agricultural and industrial products over the same period.

The increase in the rate of growth during the second period is due, basically, to the extraordinary expansion of in-

TABLE 3
RATES OF GROWTH IN BRAZIL

Period	*Agricultural Production*	*Industrial Production*	*Gross Product*
1947–1961	4.6	9.6	6.1
1957–1961	4.8	12.7	7.0

dustrial output. As the output of consumer goods grew at the same rate as the gross product, we must deduce that the basic factor in growth was the rapid expansion of the capital goods industries that occurred during these years. In effect, between 1955 and 1961, while industrial production as a whole grew about 80 percent, the steel industry increased 100 percent, the mechanical industries around 125 percent, the electrical and communications industries 380 percent, and the transportation equipment industry around 600 percent.

A clear idea of the structural changes in Brazilian economy in the 'fifties can be gathered from the figures given in table 4.

The rapid postwar growth of the Brazilian economy affected the relative position of Brazil within the Latin Amer-

TABLE 4
ANNUAL RATES OF CHANGE BETWEEN 1950–1951 AND 1960–1961

	Percent
Imports	3.3
Production for the domestic market	6.0
Imports of manufactured consumer goods	–4.5
Total consumption	5.3
Imports of equipment	3.5
Imports of raw materials	6.3
Industrial output	9.3

ican framework. In effect, while Brazil's share of Latin American production was 28 percent in 1950, about 40 percent of the increase that took place from 1950 to 1961 was owing to increased Brazilian production. In this period, the annual rate of growth for Latin America (excluding Brazil) was 40 percent, or approximately 1 percent per capita. The latter rate is about one-third of the Brazilian rate over the same period.

FARMING AND STOCK-RAISING

In the postwar period, the annual rate of growth of the farming and cattle industries was relatively high, i.e., 4.6 percent. In the most recent period, 1957–1961, this rate has gone up to 4.8 percent. However, if we take into account the increase in population and, even more important, the growth of urbanization, we must admit that this increase is cancelled out,

TABLE 5
BRAZIL'S SHARE OF LATIN AMERICAN AGRICULTURAL EXPORTS

	1950	1957	1958	1959	1960	1961
			(million tons)			
Coffee						
Brazil	1071	1409	1860	2640	1800	2280
Latin America	1900	2457	2930	3787	2931	3471
Brazilian percentage	56.4	57.3	63.5	69.7	61.4	65.7
Sugar						
Brazil	1401	2714	3004	3108	3319	3354
Latin America	9577	12655	13547	14022	14636	14790
Brazilian percentage	14.6	21.4	22.2	22.2	22.7	22.7
Cotton (fiber)						
Brazil	393	397	377	474	555	625
Latin America	913	1232	1347	1234	1397	1489
Brazilian percentage	43.0	32.2	28.0	38.4	39.7	42.0

TABLE 6
BRAZIL'S PRODUCTION OF BASIC FOOD PRODUCTS

	1950	1957	1958	1959	1960	1961	1962
	(thousand tons)						
Manioc	12532	15443	15380	16575	17613	18058	19843
Corn	6024	7763	7270	7787	8672	9036	9580
Rice	3218	4072	3829	4101	4795	5392	5557
Beans	1248	1582	1454	1550	1731	1745	1709
Sweet potatoes	833	1086	1052	1188	1283	1356	1454
Potatoes	707	999	1017	1025	1113	1080	1134
Wheat	532	781	589	611	713	545	680
Peanuts	117	192	308	357	408	584	648
Soybeans	—	122	131	152	206	272	345

agricultural products being in relatively short supply. This is proved by the more rapid increase of prices for agricultural products, these having gone up by about 50 percent over this period, as compared to industrial products.

The tables show the evolution of Brazilian agricultural export products compared with Latin America as a whole.

As regards the country's basic food products, growth was on the whole favorable, as we can see from table 6.

Meat production has on the whole gone up less than agricultural production. The figures refer to the population of the principal species.

TABLE 7
LIVESTOCK IN BRAZIL

	1950	1957	1958	1959	1960	1961	1962
	(thousand head)						
Cattle	52655	69548	71420	72829	73962	76176	79078
Pigs	26059	44190	45262	46823	47944	50051	52941
Sheep	14251	20164	19921	18995	18162	19168	19718

TABLE 8
BRAZIL'S GROWTH IN THE BASIC INDUSTRIES

	1950	1957	1958	1959	1960	1961	1962
	(million barrels)						
Petroleum							
Production	0.3	10.1	18.9	23.6	29.6	34.8	33.4
Refining	—	—	48.4	53.6	63.7	77.5	101.0
	(thousand metric tons)						
Iron ore	1987	4977	5185	8908	9345	10220	10778
Manganese ore	196	918	882	1033	999	1016	1171
Coal	1959	2073	2240	2330	2330	2390	2508
Steel ingots	789	1470	1659	1866	2282	2493	2625
Cement	1386	3376	3790	3841	4474	4711	5039
Electric power							
	(thousand kilowatts)						
Installed capacity	1883	3444	3993	4115	4800	5205	5783
	(million kilowatt-hours)						
Production	7000	16963	19766	21108	22865	24405	26895
	(units produced)						
Automobiles	—	30700	61129	96243	133078	145674	191194
Tractors	—	—	—	—	—	4056	7586

INDUSTRY

The growth of industrial production was exceptionally intense throughout the whole postwar period. In the basic industries, this growth was particularly remarkable, as can be seen from the figures in the table.

During the whole of the 1947–1961 period, the average annual rate of growth of industrial production was 9.6 percent, i.e., 50 percent higher than that of the gross product. During the period 1957–1961, the annual rate of growth of industrial production has gone up to 12.7 percent, i.e., a difference of more than 80 per cent of the rate of growth of the gross product. Taking into account the fact that the production of manufactured consumer goods grows in relation to the replacement of imports and the increase of income available for consumption, that the process of replacing imported consumer goods was already quite advanced in the middle of the 'fifties, and that the demand for manufactured consumer goods generally shows a relation between 1.0 and 1.2 with respect to the growth of the product, we must deduce that the great difference between the rate of growth of the industrial production and that of the gross product (1.5 to 1 for the whole of the 1947–1961 period) expresses a process of change in the entire structure of the national economy. The jump of that difference from 1.8 to 1 in the period 1957–1961 indicates an intensification of these structural changes.

Current Problems

The social tensions that characterize the development of Brazil at the present time can only be explained within the framework of a deeper analysis of the national historical process. In general, it is accepted that social tensions tend to become more acute during periods of stagnation in any country. In Brazil, however, these tensions have apparently been aggravated by the intensification of development, or, at least, have accompanied this intensification. To explain this contradiction, we must bear in mind that the Brazilian institutional framework, which has, for the most part, endured up to the present time, was established as the result of the secular process of growth of an economy almost entirely based on great estates producing primary goods for export. Only three decades ago, the ruling class in Brazil was still almost entirely composed of the great landowners. The urban population was small, and had limited political expression. The tradition of slavery, which had lasted almost four centuries, gave way to a system in which labor relations were marked by a profound social differentiation between employer and employee. The representative system, consolidated during the monarchical regime and continuing under the Republic until 1930, operated almost entirely from the top down, since the executive power was entrusted with both the nomination of candidates for the legislature and the supervision of election results.

After 1930, the old semi-feudal agrarian structure, which served as a prop of the political system, began to break up. With the decline of agricultural export activities and the development of an urban industrial sector, new bases for political power emerged. The class of industrial entrepreneurs, and workers' and employees' organizations, began increasingly to participate in political movements. However, the effective participation of these new forces has been reduced by the rigidity of the old institutional framework that assures the control of a substantial fragment of power by groups representing the old structure. The federal system, providing for an excessively large representation in congress, particularly in the senate, of the less developed regions, has contributed to the difficulties of the transition process. On the other hand, the incorporation of the working masses into full political activity is made more difficult by the law that gives voting rights only to the literate minority of this class.

In its present phase, Brazil is therefore a country in transition. The greatest obstacle to a gradual transition lies in the fact that the most urgent reform—which would give the system a greater capacity for self-adaptation, and make it easier to introduce further reforms—happens to be the most difficult to introduce. This, of course, is political reform, aimed at increasing the representativeness of the organs that act in the name of the people. Once this higher degree of effective democracy has been achieved, other changes in the institutional framework can be introduced without excessive tensions in the political system. It has been hitherto impossible to find a way of effecting this basic reform, so that the other institutional changes required by development have been made very slowly and in a climate of tremendous tension.

The structural changes that have already taken place in the Brazilian economy indicate that the decisive phase of its industrialization process has been approached. The basic dynamic impulse can now be internally generated, since the country is now able to produce most of the equipment needed to maintain a high rate of growth. The fact that Brazil is approaching this industrial maturity is particularly significant because of its extraordinary potential for industrial growth. In effect, Brazil's resources of raw materials and energy, which are only just beginning to be fully known, open up exceptional prospects. This enormous potential is only waiting for the country to find the definitive path for its development.

By the end of the present decade, the Brazilian population will number almost 100 million inhabitants, with about 50 million people living in the urban areas. If structural tensions have been overcome, paving the way for recuperation by means of a high rate of growth, by that time the country will have reached full industrial maturity. As the principal nation of the tropical area, Brazilian culture and technology will obviously claim worldwide attention. The democratic attitude in the ethnic formation of the people will make it easier for Brazilian values to be spread abroad, giving the country an important role among the emerging nations of the tropical world.

The experience of recent years demonstrates, however, that structural obstacles are looming increasingly large. The rate of growth began to decline in 1962, and the period 1963–1964 has been shown to be a phase of stagnation, the first since the war. If structural obstacles proved difficult to overcome in conditions of development, the difficulties to be faced in the present stagnant phase will be even greater. We must therefore expect an aggravation of the Brazilian crisis. The economic foundations of this crisis will be analyzed in greater detail in the following chapter.

8

Economic Causes of the Present Crisis

The Transition Toward Industrial Capitalism in Brazil

Brazilian development in the twentieth century is distinguished by the advent and progressive predominance of factors formative of an industrially based capitalist economy. This was a relatively slow process, with peculiar characteristics that distinguish it from the classical model of capitalist development outlined in a previous chapter. The economy that existed in Brazil, and has gradually been disintegrating as industrial capitalism takes over, was a colonial type economy; in other words, it was strongly dependent on external ties. Unlike the classical feudal economy, against which European capitalism took its stand—first as a commercial revolution, and only much later as an industrial economy—the Brazilian colonial economy bore strong traces of mercantile development, presenting itself as a self-justifying system because of its capacity for growth.

Brazilian colonial economy was essentially a projection of expanding western capitalism. The search for primary products, and the desire for a productive application of capital on the part of the capitalist powers, created the dynamic factors that permitted waves of migration to Brazil, extensive occupation of its territory, creation of an underlying structure of public services and, indirectly, urbanization and formation of the nucleus for a domestic market.

The first three decades of the present century can be regarded as a transition phase in which the dynamism of the external factors had been weakened, without the growth of awareness of the nature of the changes that were taking place. In earlier periods, the country had already faced similar situations, when the factors responsible for its growth had been exhausted and long periods of economic lethargy had followed. This happened after the expulsion of the Dutch, with the loss of the sugar monopoly, when the Northeast entered a prolonged period of depression. Similarly, the exhaustion of the gold economy caused a lengthy depression of the central-southern region at the end of the eighteenth century, which lasted through the first decades of the nineteenth. The impact of the second depression was, however, partially cancelled by the recovery of sugar and the development of agriculture in the Maranhão region, with the impulse given to the market for agricultural products during the period stretching from the American Revolution to the Napoleonic Wars.

The first three decades of the twentieth century are marked by the coffee crisis in Brazil. The withholding of large stocks, and the valorization schemes supported by overseas financiers, were started during the first years of the century. However, the short-lived Amazonian rubber boom, which created the conditions for the Murtinho miracle,[1] together with the development of other export items of limited importance, such as cocoa and maté, made it impossible to realize the true gravity of the crisis gripping the national economy. It is perfectly understandable that the ruling class of the period should have thought of economic policy only in terms of an effort to "mend" the country, to reestablish the schemes that had formerly worked. During these three decades, Brazil's exports increased less than its population, and even less than its urban population, which was more closely committed to the export monetary economy. On the other hand, a growing share of export earnings was being used to meet the external debt, contracted chiefly to support the coffee valorization policy. The external debt dominated the whole framework of public finance; and the central problem of government was the fluctuation of the foreign exchange rates. Even in the middle of the 'twenties, a president of the Republic, preoccupied with a decline in the foreign exchange reserves, decreed that all federal public works should be called to a halt, since he was convinced that the national welfare was much more dependent on regular service of the external debt than on the country's level of employment.

After 1930, the coffee economy began to disintegrate. The crisis in the world market that began in 1929, coupled with the great wave of overproduction that reached its peak in 1931, caused a collapse of the coffee economy, which continued in a state of complete depression for the next fifteen years. The political movement of 1930 renewed the top layers of the ruling class by removing the groups most directly linked to the export economy. New ruling elements from areas less committed to overseas markets (such as Rio Grande do Sul) initiated a policy which, although it did not follow any consciously established aim, was at least based on a closer contact with reality and was less conditioned by the ideological systems that prevailed among rulers from the coffee-growing areas. Thus, a phase of "political realism" was initiated, in which an attempt was made to counter severe ills with drastic cures, without overmuch concern to maintain a consistent attitude, or any real awareness of the consequences of these actions.

It was during this period of political realism that industrial capitalism was established and consolidated. It would be wrong to suppose that the dominance of the industrial capitalist class in Brazil was caused by open conflict with the existing ruling classes. In fact, industrial capitalism began to make its first significant progress when the colonial economy had already begun to disintegrate, its leaders having abandoned a consistent ideological position to dedicate themselves to improvised political opportunism.

During the transition from a colonial to an industrial

economy in Brazil, there was no shift in the archaic superstructure despite the developmental process of new productive forces with interests seeking expression in the political sphere. Classic revolutions of the French type occurred after periods of great development, during phases of remarkable economic vigor and no less remarkable administrative and financial disorder, as a consequence of the ruling group's inability to grasp the problems created by the new economic reality. It is the superseded ruling classes, unable to govern a rapidly changing society, who, by their errors and omissions, aggravate the tensions that provoke revolutionary outbursts. The Paris Commune only emerged three years after the Fall of the Bastille, as an expression of popular resentment against governments that continued to try to come to terms with a court whose sole aim was to betray the Revolution.

In the Brazilian case, however, the crisis had not resulted from antagonism between the developing new productive forces and the superseded ideologies of the ruling class. The decadent colonial economy did not encounter any rivalry from the formation of the new system. Its decadence was simply a reflection of the weakening of external stimuli. There was no endogenous development in the country that conflicted with the interests of the exploring sector. As a colonial economy, the Brazilian economy was one of the ramifications of world capitalism whose centers were located in Europe and the United States. Its crises and problems were merely adaptations to the new conditions that arose in the dynamic centers of capitalist economy.

After 1930, with the collapse of the colonial economy, the country entered a phase of irreversible structural changes, whose far-reaching consequences would only be realized much later. The policy of defending coffee was carried out despite the impossibility of gaining any external support. Huge stocks of coffee were built up and about 80 million bags were destroyed in a ritual of political realism that lasted more than a decade. The aim of this policy was to provide relief for the coffee growers by transferring to the bulk of the population the losses that would otherwise be concentrated in the coffee-growing sector. The practical effects, however, were much wider, since what happened was that the level of employment in the other sectors was defended although the capacity to import was declining. Thus, one of the side products of the "realistic" defense of the coffee growers was the creation of highly favorable conditions for investment in the home market. From this point, the industrialization process leading to the final collapse of the colonial economy, already in a state of crisis, began. In this way, industrialization, which supported the new capitalist class, was caused by the crisis in the colonial economy, and by the way in which this economy had attempted to defend itself, and was not itself a causative factor in this crisis.

During the transitional phase that began in 1930, the classes that ruled the country were essentially the same as those of the preceding period. Many years were to pass before the changes that had taken place in the economic structure were recognized and a policy aimed at consolidating industrialization needed. Nevertheless, the political opportunism of the new rulers, far less rigid in their ideological outlook than the men of Minas and São Paulo who had formerly governed the Republic, indirectly paved the way for industrialization. Since then, the Brazilian economy has not depended on external impulses for its growth. A dynamic center, based on the domestic market, has been created in the country.

The period that began in 1930 must be considered on the whole as the period when the industrial system was implanted. This implantation, however, presents individual characteristics that must be taken into account. In its initial phase, Brazilian industrialization essentially involved the establishment of industries to satisfy an existing demand, that is, to replace imports. Only at a more advanced stage did the problem arise of satisfying the demand created by development itself, particularly the demand for capital goods.

Interaction of Accumulative and Inflationary Processes

The formation of industrial capitalism in Brazil obviously required an ample accumulation process, the analysis of which is necessary to explain its capacity for growth. In its first stage, industrialization was basically a process of replacing imports. The maintenance of a high level of income during conditions of depression in the external sector increased the competitive capacity of existing industrial activities, which were established at a time when they could be indirectly protected by the successive depreciations of Brazilian currency.

We must bear in mind that these depreciations operated as a mechanism for socializing the losses of the exporting sector during periods of depression for primary products in the world markets. Between 1929 and 1937, while imports declined by 23 percent, industrial output increased by 50 percent. This expansion was made possible by an extensive utilization of existing capacities and by importing a certain amount of equipment, including secondhand equipment offered at reduced prices during the worldwide depression.

Increased output due to more intensive use of the capacity of equipment and the labor force (working two or three shifts) was paralleled by a relative rise in the prices paid by the consumer, whose needs had hitherto been satisfied by imports. In this way, there was a simultaneous increase in production and relative prices, allowing for a greater rate of return. The first wave of inflation, caused by the purchase of coffee stocks for accumulation and destruction, operated as a mechanism for transferring income to the industrial sector, creating the conditions for ample accumulation. This accumulation was reinforced by the spontaneous transfer of resources from the exporting sector, whose rate of profit was on the decline.

During the last three decades, industrialization has persistently been supported by the convergence of these two factors: substitution for imports, and transference of resources caused by inflation. Each factor has gone through different phases but has remained inseparable from the process of industrialization, a clear indication that the transition is still under way.

Replacement of imports in its first phase was simply a question of filling a gap. In view of the collapse of the import capacity, imported goods had become relatively more expensive. Domestic products, hitherto neglected because of inferior quality or higher price, began to be acceptable. In other cases, demand was deflected to similar products, as was the case with the overseas tourism that gave way to domestic tourism. Expansion of certain domestic lines of production had consequences on the composition of the demand for imports, since it created the need to import intermediary products, raw materials, and equipment. Once the import capacity had become stagnant, pressure created by the new demand for imported products pushed up the prices of products purchased abroad, thus permitting the import substitution process to continue. As the import capacity remained depressed for a considerable length of time, the substitution process, once under way, tended to continue. At first, the more easily manufactured non-durable consumer goods were replaced. This was followed by replacement of durable consumer goods, certain intermediary products, and even a fair amount of equipment. Nevertheless, this process would tend to reach a relative saturation point. Some products are hard to replace, such as wheat, coking coal, or sulphur; substitution of others requires a great effort or would be too time-consuming, as in the case of crude oil, copper, and heavy equipment. When this point of relative saturation is reached, substitution ceases to be a dynamic factor and becomes a serious handicap to accumulation. Thus, an obstacle to development is created that can only be overcome by the development of an autonomous technology and an independent supply of equipment characteristic of full economic development. Only when an economy can base itself on domestic industry for effecting investments, is it able to overcome the obstacles created by the import capacity, or at least to reduce this limitation to manageable proportions.

If the existence of a demand to be met was the necessary condition in order for the crisis in the colonial economy to give rise to a rapid process of industrialization, it was nevertheless an insufficient condition. Accumulation was basically supported by an inflationary process that in the last three decades has assumed various forms. Inflation is a process of redistributing income, variously caused, but always operating for the benefit of groups linked to investment. In its initial phase, the government, in order to protect the coffee industry, initiated a vast program of building up stocks of coffee, financing this by issuing paper currency. This policy, as we have seen, indirectly benefited the small industrial sector and created the conditions for its rapid growth. Real income, which was redistributed as the result of inflation, was, in this phase, itself created by inflation. It was not simply a question of renewed economic activity similar to what happens in a developed capitalist economy during a phase of cyclic recovery. In view of the insufficiency of the import capacity, simple maintenance of the employment level involved creating an internal imbalance that expressed itself in an increase of the price level. Nevertheless, the economy was operating at a far higher level of activity than it had before inflation. The resulting increase in income was to a large extent concentrated by inflation, to the advantage of the industrial sector.

The transfers of income made possible by the more effective utilization of productive capacity were, however, only a phenomenon of the first inflationary phase of the 'thirties. Immediately afterwards, inflation began to operate in other directions. The substitution process itself, by creating pressure for an increase in the relative prices of previously imported goods, also acted as a mechanism for transferring income in favor of the industrialists. Nevertheless, it was through the foreign exchange policy that inflation operated most profoundly as a mechanism for transferring income. By stabilizing the exchange rate and introducing selective control of imports, and, at the same time, increasing the level of domestic prices, conditions were created for the great transfers of income that favored industrial accumulation in the postwar period.

It cannot be said that there was a conscious policy aimed at increasing the profits of the industrial sector, even though this was the ultimate result. During the war, and in the years immediately following, the stabilization of the foreign exchange rate merely permitted an increase of value for the reserves accumulated in the hands of the government and business firms. This increase in value was, however, to a large extent nullified by the sudden rise in price levels in the international markets that occurred between 1945 and 1948. Massive transfers of income occurred between 1949 and 1953, when internal prices went up at an average annual rate of 15 percent and the foreign exchange rate remained stable. This was only possible, however, thanks to the extraordinary improvement in Brazil's terms of trade in this period. In this way, the real income redistributed by inflation in favor of the industries importing raw materials, intermediary products, and equipment at subsidized prices, was created abroad, and was transferred to Brazil through the mechanism of the terms of trade.

In the two cases referred to, inflation played a basic role in the process of Brazilian industrialization. In the first case, without inflation, the level of income would have been much lower and the level of investment lower still. The rate of growth would therefore have been much smaller and perhaps even negative. In the second case, inflation played a major role in raising the investment rate and concentrating investments in the industrial sector. Without inflation, the rate of growth would certainly have been lower. In addition to these two cases, inflation operated as a mechanism for redistributing income through the banking system. During the last two decades, the official banks have been placing substantial sums of resources at the disposal of private groups, at negative rates of interest, their coffers being replenished by new emissions of paper currency. In this case, the transfers operate as a highly regressive tax, the proceeds of which amounted virtually to simple donations made to private groups. These donations, however, are not destined exclusively for the industrial sector. They equally benefit agricultural and commercial activities, and thus represent an indirect increase in the profit rate. That is to say, they operate as a mechanism for limiting consumption in favor of the capitalist class.

In the first two cases referred to above, inflation redistributed the real income which had been formed partially as a consequence of the inflationary process itself, or outside the economic system. It was, therefore, a dynamic redistribution. In the third case, inflation operated on existing income, and initiated a series of reactions that tended to cancel its initial effect. Since it was an attempt to restrict mass consumption, it provoked a compensatory reaction on the part of the masses and led inexorably to the creation of a spiral of prices and costs. This inflationary spiral could be stopped only if other factors created a rise in the rate of growth. If, however, the action of these other factors was for any reason eliminated, inflation would have to degenerate into a sterile process. Nevertheless, we must recognize that the combination of inflation of the first two types and the third type, during certain periods, operated as a mechanism favorable for accumulation, creating high rates of growth, particularly in the industrial sector. On the one hand, additional resources for industrial development were channeled (those deriving from the improved terms of trade, for instance); on the other, consumption was restricted as a result of the persistent rise in the level of prices. Real wages could be controlled, and the improvement in productivity concentrated in business profits.

Weakening of Dynamic Factors

Have the dynamic factors responsible for the industrialization process of the last three decades continued to operate? Has the Brazilian economy reached that degree of structural differentiation at which capitalist economies necessarily begin generating their own development? If we could answer these two questions in the affirmative, then we could declare that the transition from a colonial economy to an industrial capitalist economy has been fully achieved. The immediate prospects for development and the political options that face the country at the present time will be better understood, if we can elucidate these questions.

We have seen that industrialization was directly based on the system of replacing imports with domestic material, and that accumulation in the industrial sector was directly bound up with the various waves of inflation. Inflation was not the primary factor in development, but it operated as a brake on structures and transferred resources, to the most dynamic sectors, by taxing the consumer and causing an increase in investments. We must, however, recognize the fact that the dynamic possibilities for replacing imports have already been exhausted. At the present time, investments intended for the substitution of domestic products for imports are among the most difficult to obtain. They are all highly capitalized investments involving long maturation periods. Therefore, the capacity to import has become a genuine obstacle to development. This obstacle has become even more formidable since 1955, as a result of serious deterioration in the terms of trade. In the effort to overcome the difficulty, the country has been led to incur an increasing external debt. The medium-term effects of this debt inevitably made themselves felt, causing the import capacity to shrink even further in order to service the large debt, thus creating a cumulative circular process in which measures to circumvent the barrier of the import capacity tended to strengthen this barrier.

From the moment when the terms of trade began to deteriorate, the only remaining source that could feed inflation without provoking a spiral of prices and costs was lost. The government had to abandon the taxation of exports implicit in the difference of exchange rates, and cover the lack of reserve funds by further emissions of paper currency. Subsidization for importers of equipment, through the "cost of exchange," [2] was gradually eliminated. Thus, inflation ceased to be an effective mechanism for the redistribution of income, and more and more became simply a sterile game of passing the buck. And in proportion as it becomes increasingly sterile, the inflationary spiral is increasingly aggravated. The last resort lies in the credit provided by the official banks, whose lines of credit become highly prized privileges to be fought over. However, the reaction of the working masses becomes increasingly rapid, and adjustments to earnings have to be made at increasingly shorter intervals. Under present conditions, when salary adjustments are made at ever shorter intervals, losses incurred from wage disputes are probably greater than the gains still made from inflation by the capitalist class. And while gains remain concentrated in certain sectors, losses are spreading to an increasing number of sectors. Thus, in its totally sterile phase, inflation is no longer harmful merely to the community as a whole and the working class in particular, but becomes harmful also to the class that originally benefited from it.

Exhaustion of the factors supporting the industrialization process apparently occurred before the formation of capital had reached autonomy vis-à-vis the external supply of capital goods. And this fact would seem to indicate that the difficulties the country has recently been facing have deeper roots than was initially suspected. A good deal of evidence exists to indicate that industrialization has brought Brazil very close to the position where development becomes a cumulative circular process creating its own expansionary momentum. For Brazil, this point would have been reached when the barrier of the import capacity had been overcome. The economy would then have achieved the degree of differentiation in which planning of investments becomes a matter of economic options, without the physical limitations of a restricted import capacity. It can even be conceded that, had it not been for the worsening of the terms of trade after 1955, Brazil would have reached this decisive point somewhere in the 'sixties. However, the opportunity to join the exclusive club of the mature capitalist economies, as an autonomous national system, was apparently lost. And once lost, other forces began to operate whose effects will be increasingly felt. Thus, once the impulse for growth was checked, the mechanism that had so far been successfully used to limit control on consumption, and to sustain the accumulation process, was, as we have seen, rendered sterile. As a result, social problems have acquired a new dimension, beyond the reach of instruments that had hitherto been used with relative success.

Full differentiation of a national economic structure does not simply imply the capacity to effect investments in the form required by development. It implies, in addition, that the productive capacity can only be utilized if the rate of investment reaches a certain level. There exists, therefore, a necessary rate of growth demanded by the internal logic of the economy that tends to increase as productivity in the sector producing capital goods (which absorbs the most advanced technology) increases in relation to national production as a whole. It is this situation that occurs during the transition from underdevelopment to industrial maturity. However, to the extent that investments depend on imports in order to be effected, the operation of the import capacity determines the effective behavior of the investment level. If the import capacity barrier increases, there must be a corresponding intensification of the effort to increase savings, in order to keep up with rises in the relative prices of capital goods. Thus, conditions are created that tend to reduce the rate of growth, and this hampers the structural modifications needed to overcome the import capacity barrier.

Important consequences result from this decrease in the rate of growth. It is a well-known fact that agricultural production for the home market has been notoriously slow to respond to the demand generated by industrial development. Unlike many other countries, where agriculture commonly bore the whole weight of industrial accumulation in its early stages, in Brazil the mass of consumers in general, and the exporting agricultural sector in particular, were the mainstay of industrial accumulation. The predominance of feudal structures in agriculture, for the home market even more than for export, caused great inelasticity in the supply of food for the urban areas, which created serious obstacles to development. On the whole, the prices of manufactured products went up less than those of agricultural products intended for home consumption, which indicates that the industrial capitalist class had to allocate part of its profits to the interests tied up with the great estates. The whole process operated as if the new capitalist class was obliged to pay its feudal dues to the most retrograde sector of the old capitalist class. Once the factors that permitted rapid capitalization and high profit margins for the industrial sector had been eliminated, this tribute paid to the estate-owning groups became an increasing burden. The anachronistic agrarian structure as an obstacle to development ceased to be merely a suspicion and became a glaring reality. Nevertheless, elimination of this obstacle is no easy matter. It cannot be undertaken within the bounds of the conventional channels, along which development has moved up to the present time.

In order to understand the interrelations between the rising industrial sector and the preexisting agricultural class, we must identify the two clearly defined branches of the latter. On one side, there was the important branch of agriculture for export, mainstay of the colonial economy; on the other, there was the branch of agriculture intended for the home market, which had developed in quite different historical circumstances. The first, imbued with the mercantile spirit, traditionally maintained control of the great centers of political decision. The second was based on a semi-feudal structure with a relatively limited use of money, and confined its political activities to local issues. We have already observed that industrial development, in its early stages, was intimately bound up with the colonial economy, which hindered an ideological differentiation among the respective ruling groups. However, as industrialization called for urbanization on a wider scale, so the inadequacy of the structure of agriculture for the home market became increasingly apparent.

As the ideological position of the agricultural sector is, in general, directed toward the defense of the institutional status quo, based on its strength in the legislative power, the landowning group with the most antisocial bias always managed to move within a broad front in which its interests could be identified with those of agriculture as a whole, or even with the interests of all owners of the means of production. It was, therefore, difficult for the industrial capitalist class to become aware of the conflict of interests between industrialization and the groups who control the lands used for food production. This awakening was rendered even more difficult by the increase in social tensions caused by the decrease in the rate of growth in the early 'sixties. More aggressive action by the working masses, and the spread of social conflict to the rural areas, necessarily entailed an ideological polarization that obscured the internal contradictions of the capitalist class itself. In this way, at the very moment the agrarian problem began to penetrate the consciousness of the ruling class, the political feasibility of its solution became more remote. We must ask how the agrarian problem could have evolved in a different way, if the industrial structure had achieved full differentiation. In this case, industry would have been equipped to offer agriculture machinery and other inputs at declining prices relative to those of agricultural products. Conditions would have been created for the formation of a capitalist class in agriculture, which would force the positions of the old feudal structure. The use of advanced techniques in agriculture tends to undermine feudal structures since it requires a specialized labor force and advanced forms of organization and supervision. This internal change in agriculture has already begun in certain areas of the country. However, industrial support for agriculture is still in its early stages—the stage of supplying agricultural machinery and inputs at very high prices relative to similar goods previously imported. With the decline in the rate of industrial growth, the labor force that is absorbed outside agriculture tends to be reduced, as does the total demand for agricultural products. This discourages investment in agriculture, and reduces even further the prospect of spontaneous changes in its structure.

Another relevant aspect of the inflationary process, hitherto only implicitly referred to, is its ties with the public sector. Industrial development, particularly in the postwar period, was significantly supported by a substantial increase in public investments, or directly financed by public authority. In view of the anachronistic and obsolete nature of the country's sub-structure, which had been organized for the colonial economy, there was a pressing need for a massive effort for investment in the basic sectors: transportation, electric power, liquid fuel, steelworks, and so forth. These investments needed to be made on a wide scale by public authority, if strangulation of the industrial process was to be avoided. In view of the failure of the ruling class to awaken to the new functions of the public authority at a time of transition in the country's economy, investments in the sub-structure were effected in a more or less haphazard way in an obstacle race against successive bottlenecks. The insufficiency of overhead investments created tensions that increased the economy's vulnerability to inflation. On the other hand, there was a failure to create the conditions under which the public authority could adapt itself to fulfill its new functions. The administrative machinery grew by fits and starts under the pressure of irreversible situations. Investments of vital importance to the country and that should have been the responsibility of the public authority (in the steel and energy sectors, for instance), were without any adequate financial programming for a considerable time, and were dependent on occasional loans by the Bank of Brazil on behalf of the treasury, backed by emissions of paper currency.

With the gradual elimination of revenue derived from the differences in exchange rates, the disequilibrium of the public sector, hitherto more or less concealed, became fully evident in all its magnitude. If the federal government tried to wipe out the huge deficit in its accounts by reducing planned expenditure to the expected revenue—even allowing revenue its broadest interpretation—it would necessarily provoke a serious economic crisis, creating mass unemployment and paralyzing a large part of the basic works in progress. On the other hand, if the government tried to carry out its planned expenditure, it would be forced to resort to inflationary forms of financing the budget, throwing the whole structure of costs and prices out of gear, and thus partly frustrating its own expenditure program. In other words, the government was not institutionally equipped to carry out the task, allotted by the community, of supporting the development process. And the situation persisted because of the lack of a political basis for carrying out the fiscal reforms that would provide relief. The capitalist class, in general, insisted that the government reduce expenditure that directly or indirectly subsidized consumption, as in the case of deficits incurred in public utilities. On the other hand, the masses applied pressure to re-allocate and increase the tax burden.

The impasse in the fiscal sector has placed the government in the midst of a dilemma: to cut down on its investments and assume responsibility for hampering development, or to resort to inflation. In the latter case, its experience proved identical to that of the private sector. During the period when the redistributory mechanism of inflation was supported by increases in real income, owing to better terms of trade and expansion of physical productivity caused by rapid accumulation in the industrial sector, the government could increase its participation in the social product above that permitted by straightforward expenditure of its revenue. When the inflationary process became sterile, the government was obliged to face growing difficulties in maintaining its participation in the product, with the marginal effectiveness of emissions of paper currency growing smaller day-by-day. The need for fiscal reform became imperative. However, because of the decline in the rate of growth of the economy, there was an increase in the political difficulties involved in carrying out reforms.

Growth of Structural Tensions

If we attempted to sum up the details, outlined above, of the evolution of the Brazilian economy in this century, we could say that the colonial system had already entered a critical phase in the first decade, but that only since the early 'thirties has there been a clearly marked transition toward industrial capitalism. This transition has lasted three decades and has substantially altered the economic structure. But it has not yet permitted a perfectly differentiated industrial system, able to base itself on self-generated impulses for growth, and to adapt itself automatically to increased internal demand, and able to overcome adverse autonomous movements in external demand.

This transition is marked by the formation of a new dynamic center, created by accumulation in the industrial sector. This accumulation process was, however, based on specific circumstances that should not be ignored. The gap created by the collapse of the import capacity at a time when the level of money income was expanding or being kept up, acted as the primary force for stimulating accumulation in the industrial sector. The growth of industrial production, on the other hand, acted as a supplementary factor for exerting pressure on the import capacity, thus causing a repetition on a wider scale of the conditions that had favored the initial process of import replacement. For each wave of pressure on the import capacity, there was necessarily a corresponding rise in the general level of prices, so that development proceeded under permanently inflationary conditions. It was this connection between accumulation in the industrial sector and inflation that permitted the substantial increase in income caused by development throughout the period. It particularly permitted the increase caused by the improved terms of trade between 1949 and 1955 to be appropriated for investment, both in the industrial sector itself and in the public sector.

Thus, for a fairly long period, inflation was bound up with the dynamic factors that were responsible for an increase in the investment rate, and the concentration of these investments in the industrial sector. Inflation allowed appropriation of the increase in income by the industrialists and concentration of investments in the dynamic sector. In turn, investments guaranteed a further increase in income, which could continue to be appropriated by the capitalists, thanks to inflation. This process, however, finally encountered a barrier in the form of the reduced import capacity which, once the possibilities of replacing imports with domestic goods had been exhausted, tended to become a growing obstacle to the maintenance of a high level of investment. In view of the increased difficulties in substituting imports, pressure on the import capacity resulted chiefly in the rise of the relative cost of equipment and other imported capital goods, with a consequent fall in the rate of investment.

The process we have just described was aggravated by the deterioration in the terms of trade after 1955. This led to a compensatory effort which increased the external debt and which created, in time, an untenable situation in the balance of payments, similar to the situation that had resulted from the coffee "valorization" policy. Once the primary factors that had permitted rapid accumulation in the industrial sector had ceased to act (substitution for imports, improved terms of trade), the effort to keep up a high rate of growth simply through the mechanism of inflation became increasingly less effective. Inflation ceased to act as a mechanism for concentrating the increase in real income, and became progressively an effort to redistribute existing income. This effort became more and more sterile in proportion as the income ceased to grow.

The structural problems of a transitional economy became more apparent with the decline in the rate of growth. The sectors of the ruling class that had been demanding increased participation in the product, supported by a semi-feudal agrarian structure, were revealed in their true antisocial light as soon as the rate of growth of the product decreased. A widening circle of groups of opinion became aware that the possibilities for development were being hampered by the activities of groups supported by an anachronistic structure, who were helping themselves to an appreciable portion of the increase in the product. As a result of the activities of these groups, the masses were being subjected to permanent rationing of essential agricultural products through persistent rises in relative prices. Another structural problem that became equally apparent to widespread groups of opinion with the weakening of growth, was the government's incapacity to find adequate financial backing for the investments for which it was responsible, and which are vital for the actual process of development. Once inflation had become sterile, the government was called upon to reduce its participation in the product, and this it has only managed to do, up to the present time, by cutting down on its investments. This curtailment of investments was to have immediate negative effects on growth, and in the long run, on the removal of the structural obstacles, in view of the nature of public investments.

In short, we can say that the process of formation of industrial capitalism in Brazil encountered obstacles of a structural nature that seem to be difficult to overcome within the present institutional framework and by the means the ruling classes are accustomed to use. With regard to both the external sector and the agricultural and fiscal sectors, there are obvious contradictions in the way in which the economy tends to operate under present conditions, and the requirements for the maintenance of a high level of investment. Only the intervention of unforeseeable factors, such as a sudden improvement in the terms of trade, could for a time alter the present tendencies. In the absence of such factors, everything indicates that the current tendency for the rate of growth to decline will continue, and that structural obstacles still prevail against the dynamic impulses.

Is Brazilian society equipped to overcome the difficulties that now stand in the path of the country's economic development, or will the solution be imposed by the pressure of events, once structural tensions become socially unbearable? We have already observed that industrial capitalism evolved without any conflict between its leaders and the ruling groups in power who represented the colonial economy. Protection of the interests of the coffee growers even served as the basis for the early stages of the industrialization process and, at the right moment, this process offered an alternative use for capital that could no longer find an outlet in the exporting sector, where it had been formed. On the other hand, the impulse given to the economy by industrial accumulation created an alternative market for important sections of the agricultural sector. The semi-feudal agricultural structure permitted not only the maintenance of a high level of concentration of income in favor of the landowning class, but also the transference to agriculture of part of the industrial sector's increased productivity, through a persistent rise in relative agricultural prices. Thus, although the improvement in the terms of trade was channeled in favor of industry, industry gave back to agriculture more than it took by creating a bigger home market, and through a steady increase in the relative price of the agricultural products in the domestic market. Occasional conflicts of interest within the ruling class resulted much more from the persistence of outgrown ideological forms among certain class leaders than from any facts based on objective reality.

In short, Brazil did not experience the type of bourgeois revolution that characterized the development of industrial capitalism in Europe up to the middle of the last century. This is at least partly because of a particular aspect of Brazil's historical evolution. The institutional framework, throughout the country's one hundred and fifty years of political independence, has been relatively advanced, at least from the formal point of view. Brazilians always held a very high opinion of their country, and in drawing up their constitutions they were more interested in not lagging behind the more advanced countries than in social reality and the degree of development of their national structures. This alienation had its historical advantages, for, in moments of crisis, it was always possible to find solutions in elements of the institutional framework that had remained unused and without any effective regulations. This historical circumstance mitigated the inertia peculiar to institutional patterns.

It cannot be claimed that conflicts do not exist between the interests of the groups directly involved in industrialization and those mainly supported by the old agrarian structure. However, there is no conflict of basic interests, since agriculture is also dependent on industrial accumulation once its chief market is domestic. This is why the leading elements of industrial capitalism have not realized that the parasitism of the semi-feudal agrarian sector tends to hamper the industrialization process. However, far from involving a simple redistribution of the surplus, the activities of the semi-feudal agrarian groups have the effect of hardening the economic system, strangling industry by means of an extremely inelastic food supply. This real problem, however, does not produce any ideological echoes in the ruling class, in view of the aggravation of more widespread problems that lead the capitalist groups to lend each other mutual support.

The conflict between the need for increased investments by the public sector, and the resistance to increased participation in the national product by this sector, evokes even less of an ideological echo in the ruling class. As in the previous case, the ruling agrarian sector, by resisting any attempt to make it contribute to the public revenue, is a factor for the creation of serious structural inflexibility. But, since the industrial class has failed to become aware of its conflicts with the agrarian class, it has no reason to judge this class on an independent scale of values. On the contrary, the anti-interference attitude of the agrarian groups has tended to spread among the leading elements of the industrial class, without any awareness of the contradiction that exists between such an attitude and the genuine interests of industrialization itself.

As far as the problem created by the import barrier is concerned, the possibility of an awakening of consciousness on the part of the ruling class has been equally limited, both in what concerns the long-term tendency for a relative decline in the import capacity, and in the most rational social form of using this capacity. The first tendency is owing to a simple observable fact: world trade in primary products grows less than the population of underdeveloped countries, and these products are subject to increasing competition from substitutes provided by technology, which operates in favor of the developed countries. Hence the long-term tendency for the terms of trade to deteriorate to the detriment of the underdeveloped countries, who are called upon to share among themselves an import capacity that becomes increasingly restricted. Only full industrial development that would allow the country to become integrated into the currents of growing international trade in manufactured goods, will permit the overcoming of this obstacle, created by the narrowness of the import capacity. But, as industrial development itself is restricted by the limitation of the import capacity, the possibilities of breaking this vicious circle tend to be reduced in proportion as control is lost over the utilization of the import capacity.

In view of the strategic importance that this factor came to occupy in the development process, it is understandable that foreign economic policy should have become of utmost significance for the country. We can say without exaggeration that self-determination, or lack of it, in this sector became the crucial problem of the present consolidation stage of the industrialization process. However, the historical conditions of development at the transitional phase we have been analyzing lacked the formation of a ruling class that strengthened its power through a progressive realization of positions that conflicted with the interests of other dominating groups. On this question, as on others, historical conditions acted as a factor for hindering the formulation of a long-term policy. There was, therefore, no specific legal discipline to take into account the potential conflicts between the interests of foreign groups controlling capital within the country, and those related to national development itself. The question was left to the law of survival of the fittest. The international groups, because of their privileged positions as the possessors of financial power, organizational capacity, and administrative experience, and with their easy access to more advanced techniques and publicity methods, were in an extremely strong position. They could bring under their control increasing sections of the newly formed industrial economy at a relatively low cost in terms of their own investment.

The new industrial capitalist class, lacking experience and any real foresight, generally found that the line of least resistance was to make concessions to the foreign groups as a solution of their immediate problems. From the point of view of the business interests concerned, this was often the most rational attitude. But from the national point of view, the cumulative effect of these individual decisions was only fully apparent at a much later date. In this way, an industrial economy of high and increasing foreign exchange inputs was created in conflict with the present and foreseeable possibilities of the import capacity, and completely directed toward patterns of consumption that do not correspond to the country's degree of development. Because of the action of foreign groups, even the sectors in which the contribution of foreign technology was completely dispensable or completely superfluous for social welfare, tended to increase their operating requirements in foreign currency. As inflation allowed foreign groups to appropriate a considerable share of national savings at negative rates of interest, and as the exchange policy favored foreign enterprises by allowing the reintroduction, at a favorable exchange rate, of the profits they had made in the country and remitted abroad, there was a widespread denationalization process in the economy, which led inevitably to external strangulation, independent of the action of other factors.

With the exhaustion of import substitution and the increase of the external barrier, the country realized its precarious position for the rational utilization of its import capacity in the interests of development. A conflict was therefore created between the broader interests of national development, and the individual interests of thousands of foreign-controlled enterprises, operating with more or less irreducible costs of foreign currency. The industrial capitalist class, closely bound up with the foreign groups in whom it had always found the key to the solution of its immediate problems, is not in a position to grasp the nature and seriousness of the problem. It is still commonly supposed that it could be solved by "regaining confidence" abroad, and so attracting a new inflow of foreign capital, as if the conflict would not inevitably tend to be aggravated when the future repeated the events of the past. In the present situation, in order to meet the liabilities of the past, either the financial costs in exchange or the fixed-term debits, imports would have to be cut by half. This is surely the most acute internal contradiction in Brazilian development at its present stage. It is also the problem for which the ruling class is least prepared to find a solution, since this would involve equipping the public authority for complex and multifarious action, and this would conflict with its most irremovable ideological motivations.

Impasse and Probable Options

The fact that the ruling class is not equipped to become fully aware of the problems of the present phase of development in the national economy does not alter the problems in themselves, but conditions the solutions that can be found for them. This inability to come to grips with reality is, in itself, a clear indication that the solution of these problems in some way transcends the operational capacity of the ruling class, and must therefore emerge from the interaction of more widespread forces.

The country's economy, at the mercy of a series of structural constrictions, is, by the very nature of its problem, in an unstable situation. The primary forces of development—population growth, urbanization, desire for improved living conditions expressed in the government's ambitious plans for expenditure and in social movements—are piling up like the potential energy in the waters of a river that has been dammed. The disturbing action of these primary forces tends to increase with the reduction in the economy's rate of growth. We have seen that this reduction led to an aggravation of the inflationary process, which indicates that these forces are seeking an outlet through an effort that is becoming increasingly sterile. However, the tensions created by these dammed up forces have led to the awakening of a wide number of groups, who have become aware that development is threatened by structural obstacles that are beyond the capacity for action by the present ruling groups.

If awareness of the basic problems to be faced is being achieved outside the institutional limits within which the ruling groups operate, and even as a result of conflict with these groups, it is perfectly obvious that the solutions to these problems will not be provided by the leaders of the ruling groups. Situations of this kind lead, almost inevitably, to the disruption of the existing balance of forces and the abandoning of conventional political methods. The awareness of the problem in some ways indicates that the stage of deadlock has been overcome, and that conditions for an effective attempt at finding a solution have been created. This may take various forms, the most common being the split within the ruling class, the most lucid minority groups taking advantage of the situation to remove those already in power by mobilizing the masses by means of a language that speaks to their aspirations. Only in very special historical circumstances has social subversion taken place at a deeper level, with immediate or progressive elimination of the ruling class and liquidation of their economic foundations.

The bids for power by minority groups of the ruling classes, with the intention of frustrating an incipient revolutionary process, create, of necessity, unstable situations. As the structural causes of tension continue to operate, and even increase, general unrest leads to cleavage within the ruling class itself, creating the climate for new bids and counterbids. The solution may be in the direction of disintegration, leading to a resumption of an open revolutionary process, or domination by a minority group who would impose a new system of compromises with the working masses, at the expense of sacrifices by some part of the ruling class.

The forms taken by revolutionary processes depend, to a large extent, on the historical conditions created by the revolution itself. It is in some ways possible to identify the factors that create a pre-revolutionary historical situation. However, it would not be similarly possible to identify the factors that condition a revolutionary process. Once the conditions have been created in which conventional political methods are abandoned; that is, once the institutional framework has been broken down, a number of forces, previously with no access to the political sphere, begin to operate. The interaction of these forces creates unforeseeable situations that make political action by conventional means more difficult. Nevertheless, the depth of the revolutionary process will always be dependent on the role played by the ruling class in the early stages. As there will probably be a cleavage within the ruling class, with one faction allying itself with new forces determined to break down the institutional framework, revolutions carry within themselves the elements for self-restraint, and nearly always limit themselves to carrying out only part of their program. If this part is not significant enough to open the door to the forces previously repressed, the revolution will have frustrated itself. In this way, once certain bonds have been broken, the society will continue to develop according to the plan that was already implicit in the forces that had been growing within it. Only exceptional historical circumstances, created by external conflict or prolonged civil wars, permitted revolutions to move toward complete social reconstruction. In any case, it would be pointless to conjecture where a revolution will lead, or to ask what social price it will have to pay. It is not our task to go beyond an analysis of the factors that condition the pre-revolutionary situation. This analysis allows us to deepen our understanding of historical reality, and equips us to make a clear and rational decision, in full knowledge of the situation.

Finally, we must point out that the pre-revolutionary situation should not be considered in terms of conventional value judgments. In itself, it means that the society is in the throes of a vigorous development, and that the forces opposing this development have been challenged. Obstacles to development do not appear at a given moment, suddenly creating a pre-revolutionary situation. They always exist and sometimes prevail against the dynamic factors, causing stagnation. Tensions indicate that stagnation has not been accepted, or in other words, that development has become socially imperative. Nor do we wish to imply that the pre-revolutionary situation inevitably leads to an open revolutionary process. By arousing an awareness of the roots of the crisis among widespread groups of the population, it leads to the emergence of a new national plan in opposition to the program of the group currently in power. The impact on public opinion can gain in strength and give rise to the conditions that lead to cleavage within the ruling class. This cleavage can lead to the abandonment of positions previously defended at all costs, starting a circular cumulative process in which reforms will, of necessity, lead to further reforms. However, between this reformist solution, which is far less costly socially, and the revolutionary outlet, with its unforeseeable consequences, there exists the same probability of mutual exclusion as between the emergence of a clear-sighted capacity on the part of the ruling class to grasp the true social interests, and their possessive attachment to the privileges they now enjoy.

9

The Revolutionary Process in the Northeast

The social changes that are presently taking place in Brazil, and in a particular form in the Northeast, deserve a more detailed analysis. Economists qualify these changes as structural but do not concern themselves directly with the specific historical processes that lead to them. They regard as more or less self-evident the fact that these changes, on the whole, take the form of intermittent or non-gradual advances, owing to the accumulation of pressures in the social structure that express themselves in terms of growing psychological tensions. They believe that the pressures tend, for this reason, to resolve themselves by provoking a disruption of the balance of forces that insures social stability.

Experience indicates that certain adjustments to the social structure, with consequences for the play of forces on which political power is based, are made only after a prolonged process of accumulating tensions. The psychological ingredient of this process is the different scales of value by which groups and social classes occasionally in conflict judge and interpret historical reality and project their aspirations. These tensions, in their turn, act as an autonomous factor on the formation process of group or class-consciousness and make it more difficult for common aspirations to be integrated into a single plan of social reconstruction. In other words: the climate of tensions itself is not very conducive to gradual solutions of a reformist type. This does not mean, however, that tensions in themselves are bad. Their existence simply indicates that the society is evolving, seeking more complex forms of organization. But we must point out that in societies organized on a basis of privilege enjoyed by groups or classes, with political power acting as the bulwark of privilege, any attempt to change the power structure tends to provoke tremendous opposition. To the extent that tensions give some idea of this resistance, they are also an indication of the community's effort to achieve the superior forms of organization called for by its material development and the aspirations of its people.

Today we possess analytical instruments that enable us to observe these processes, to identify the strategic factors in a given historical circumstance, and to formulate hypotheses about the most probable general trends. This makes us in some measure responsible for the course of events, if we are participants in this historical process. In effect, if we can go beyond a simple understanding of current events—since we are able to predict the basic trends of these events—and if we do not come out on the side of the solutions that will prove less costly socially, the least that can be said of students of the social sciences is that they served the interests of groups and classes against their own people, and that they betrayed the greatest of all responsibilities—the responsibility of intelligence.

It is as a historical process that can and must be directed, since its causes and basic trends are known, that we must speak of the Brazilian revolution. We must not see it as a movement that must, of necessity, evade control, inflicting itself as a natural phenomenon on primitive man, but rather as a change that will cost the people much less as they become aware of the forces involved, and become ready to demand from the groups who hold political power the measures that can be carried out without violence. The more widespread the knowledge of what is happening, the clearer the consciousness that the interests of the ruling groups conflict with the forces of popular social development, the lower the cost to the community for the structural changes needed. It is with the knowledge that we are living through a process which is in many ways revolutionary and which can still be directed, that we will attempt to analyze the reality of the Brazilian Northeast.

The Humid Coastal Zone

What is the Northeast as an economic and social reality? The information about the region published in the press gives a very vague idea of this reality. As numerous sections of the Northeastern ruling classes for a long time lived on federal government funds administered in an equivocal manner, a peculiar situation was created in which those groups interested in maintaining the status quo are the same ones who most dramatize the region's problems and cry out for the need for change. However, we are dealing with a dramatization based on false problems that deflects attention from the real ones. For this reason, the "droughts" have been made into the great enemy to be contended with, responsible for all the ills that torment the Northeasterner. Since it is not difficult, in any given year, to prove that there is indeed drought, as the rainfall is always irregular if we consider this semi-arid region as a whole, it has always been possible to divert popular attention to the "great enemy." On the other hand, as government action during drought "emergencies" took the form, in the end, of a distribution of money, the number of people in need of aid was naturally always very great, whatever the circumstances leading to recognition of the drought. The irresponsibility of those who exploited the drought harmed the Northeast in two ways: on the one hand it created a false image of the problems of the region, whose real possibilities for development began to be underestimated, with talk of the inevitability of its progressive abandonment; on the other, it justified in the minds of the majority of the country's rulers their neglect of the problems of the Northeast, a region to which "there was no point in sending money," since the money would in any case always be misused. To put right the false image, and to give an accurate picture of the complex reality of the region, is the first requirement for an understanding of the problem of the Northeast.

Of the Northeast's population, currently calculated at about 25 million people, more than two-thirds work on the land. And in the majority of cases, they live on the land, with almost no form of political organization. That is to say, they live not in communities made up of citizens, but as individuals making up family or neighborly units, with no political expression. In effect, for the average Northeasterner living on the land, his personal destiny is encompassed by a rudimentary community life with no political dimension. Now, a man who does not directly participate in a politically organized society does not become aware that the world in which he lives can be changed by his own personal actions. His attitude is passive or totally submissive to those in power who are, he thinks, the arbiters of good and evil. This pre-political state, in which a great part of the Northeastern people find themselves, is an essential element for understanding both the importance of local authorities and the role played by personal ties in the exercise of political power. Nevertheless, this in only one factor in a highly differentiated and already rapidly changing reality. If we wish to identify the essentials in this society, whose rudimentary organization protects all kinds of exploitation by an insignificant minority of the great majority, we must focus more closely on the objective.

Extending along almost the entire Northeast is a narrow, humid coastal strip, averaging 30 to 40 miles in width, where the bulk of the population is concentrated. In this coastal strip, the old sugar economy still exists, still preserving the general type of organization that the Portuguese introduced in the great estates of the sixteenth century. How can we sum up the production unit of the sugar region? Let us take a typical cane establishment, or "usina," comprising four to five agricultural units ("engenhos") and sheltering some 10,000 people within its frontiers. At the center is the industrial unit, producing sugar, which employs 5 to 8 percent of the estate workers; the rest of the population forms the peasant mass that plants, tends, trims, harvests, and transports the cane to the "usina." Agricultural activity is, therefore, fundamental. The great majority of the men who live on the great estate as agricultural workers had, up to 1963, no contractually defined labor relations. Nothing defined the rights that could be defended by anyone who derived his authority from a politically organized society. These masses of men live on the estate like the old feudal clients, or like people given permission to live on the land and hence called "moradores." [1] However, this permission is given on certain conditions, which can mean free labor for the landlord once or twice a week, or simply, that the tenant cannot accept any work outside the estate. For this reason they were also known as "condiceiros." [2]

The men who live on the great estate without any objectively defined labor relations constitute an extremely rudimentary community from the political point of view. Settler status is almost imcompatible with status as a citizen. The urban worker, who moves between factory and home, is aware that the norms that regulate a citizen's life are different from those that regulate his work, and this enables him to observe labor relations with a critical eye. On the large plantation, the man who leaves his house for work is simply moving from one part of the estate to another. Thus there is no aspect of his life that falls outside the system of norms that governs his working life. In this way, his experience of practical life does not allow him to develop as a citizen, or to become conscious of a responsibility for his own destiny. Every act of his life is the act of a client, the action of an element whose existence is in every respect integrated into a single great socioeconomic unit: the cane plantation. These men are hardly aware of belonging to a municipality or a district, the most rudimentary forms of political organization. Even when their dwellings are grouped together as a village, the village is attached to an "estate," and for this reason the impersonal link with a public authority loses clarity in comparison to the all-embracing presence of the private authority.

It is difficult for the city dweller, who forms part of a differentiated political society involving a large number of his activities, to grasp the psychosocial complex of the man who lives and dies on an estate and never attains the life of a political man, or citizen. The horizons of such a man are extremely limited, since the probability that he will always remain what he was born, a tenant cane cutter, is extremely high. He sees no link between social behavior and labor relations. Nor does he understand the link between his "political" behavior, in voting during elections, and his living conditions, which reflect labor relations. Whatever the results of elections, the local authorities, who are the only ones whose acts have an effect on his life, must of necessity be approved of by the groups who have something to defend, as the owners of the land, the machinery, the houses, the roads—in fact, of everything within the estate where the voter lives.

Let us now take a closer look at the activities of this rural worker. In the past, the great sugar plantation was practically self-sufficient. It depended on the outside only for reequipment and the odd consumer product, such as salt or kerosene, if we do not take into account the needs of the landowning class who were responsible for the considerable consumption of externally produced goods when living on the estate. During the period of slavery, a division of labor system operated, whereby a certain number of slaves prepared food for the whole community. Later, the mixed system of tenure prevailed. As the planting and harvesting season for food crops did not coincide with the most intense period of activity in the cane fields, a mixed system arose in which the cane worker was entitled to a small plot of land where he could plant subsistence crops. The tenant system was largely responsible for the slow social evolution of the population making its living from sugarcane. On the one hand, the system deprived the worker of any motivation for improving his living conditions. By excluding the possibility of property ownership, whether of the plot of land he worked or the house he lived in, it removed the primary incentive of any individual who works on the land. Any improvement to the hovel in which he lived, or even the planting of fruit trees, was actively discouraged, since this might create "rights" for which the tenant would have to be indemnified when it became convenient to remove him. On the other hand, the system led to the dispersion of workers within the estate. As the lands set aside for food crops were those considered the poorest, situated at the tops of hills, the tenants were given these plots, situated well apart from each other.

This dispersion made it difficult for the development of any kind of community life, minimized the influence of the strongest personalities, and hampered any exchange of ideas with the exterior. The isolated settler was thus subjected to the full force of the proprietor's authority and that of the political machine serving the interests of the landowning class.

This pattern, which prevailed after the abolition of slavery, has undergone profound changes during the last ten years, particularly in 1963. The industrialization of the country, entailing an increase in income per head and intense urbanization, created an appreciable increase in the consumption of sugar during this decade. In fact, national consumption rose from less than 30 million bags in 1953/1954 to over 46 million in 1962/1963. On the other hand, extremely favorable conditions in the world market permitted the resumption of export on a large scale, which led to an even greater increase in production than in consumption. The Northeast shared in this new prosperity, its output going up by approximately 50 percent in the last ten years. However, this increased output was achieved by the usual method of simply taking over new lands for cane production, these lands being generally inferior to those already under cultivation. As the average yield per hectare under cultivation remained stationary at about 40 tons, we must infer that the efforts made by a few planters to introduce irrigation systems and the use of fertilizers were barely sufficient to compensate for the incorporation of inferior land. This being the case, we must also deduce that there was an increase in the average costs of production, and a decrease in the rate of profit during the recent period of expansion, if we allow that the relative prices of inputs and product remained stable.

The practical consequences of the increase in production we have been considering were of two kinds. First, the pressure exerted for an extension of the acreage under cane cultivation led to the progressive elimination of areas previously used for growing food crops. Second, the tendency for a rise in real costs created heavy pressure on the workers' wages.

The extension of areas under cane cultivation had profoundly significant social and economic effects. The "morador," in a relatively short space of time, was transformed from a small sharecropper responsible for producing part of his family's food requirements, into a simple wage earner. From his confinement to an isolated hovel at the top of a hill, where his family had lived without any concept of neighborliness, he was pushed onto the edge of the road, no longer able to plant even "an inch of land" for food. He would have needed a substantial increase in wages to buy himself the foodstuffs he formerly produced. In this way, the transformation from "morador" into mere wage earner brought about a rise in labor costs, with no corresponding increase in productivity. The "morador" was a semi-seasonal worker who went back to a partial form of non-monetary subsistence economy when there was a decreased demand for his labor; this made him an extremely cheap form of labor, since the land he used for his domestic crops had no alternative economic use. When a use was found for this land, the same worker needed a much higher wage in order to survive. Pressure for an increase in wages was accompanied by the pressure of rising real production costs, owing to the incorporation of inferior land.

How can we explain the vigorous increase in sugar output during the last decade, in the adverse conditions created by the tendency for a rise in real costs? The explanation lies in the very nature of social organization in the Northeastern sugar industry. All decisions were made by the landowning class, although this class was in no position to foresee the long-term consequences of its actions. In view of growing competition from the well-capitalized and technically more advanced production of the country's southern region, any rise in relative sugar prices became a double-edged weapon, since the incentive this provided was much more effective in the south. In this way, unless costs were kept low in the Northeast, the tendency for the Northeast to lose its southern markets would inexorably continue. In order to achieve its twofold aim of increasing production while keeping real costs down, the landowning class had to use every means at its disposal to combat a rise in money wages. This struggle against a rise in wages, at a time when the workers were being pushed to the edge of the road, led to a reduction in the already extremely low living standards of the rural working class. To apprehend the full extent of the problem, we must bear in mind that, at the same time, adverse changes were taking place in the food market, with the production of food requirements in the cane district decreasing while demand increased. The surplus food production of the Agreste and the Sertão [3] zones was thus in great demand, with detrimental effects on the urban areas that had hitherto depended on these surpluses. Thus, yet another factor was added to the pressures exerted on the workers of the cane zone—the tendency for a rise in the relative prices of food.

By carrying out its policy of expanding sugar production without considering the broader socioeconomic implications of the problem, the landowning class involuntarily unleashed powerful forces that paved the way for structural changes in the whole pattern of the sugar economy. The advance of the cane fields over lands formerly used for the cultivation of food crops pushed the former tenants to the road, closer to the sources of food supply. Thus, they very soon established community relations and contacts that facilitated the emergence of local leaders. These leaders differed, but all worked toward fomenting an awakening of consciousness of the workers' common interests.

The growth of class-consciousness was stimulated by the hard conditions imposed on the workers by the landowning class, who reduced the meager standards of living below a conceivable subsistence level. Considering that the sugar economy was apparently prospering, with production increasing annually, pressure to reduce real wages served the rural masses as evidence that the landowners' prosperity was achieved at the cost of their misery. Between 1960 and 1962, when this pressure reached its peak, a peasant's daily earnings were hardly enough to buy a liter of cassava flour. This situation led a well-known French writer to arouse world opinion about the miserable conditions enforced on the peasant masses of the Northeast, calling it a case of flagrant genocide.

We must digress a moment in order to explain the extraordinary phenomenon of the Peasant Leagues, whose rapid spread has been without parallel in the history of Brazilian social movements. In the early stages of their growth, the Leagues encountered organized and violent resistance from an oligarchy whose power was similar to that of a totalitarian state. They soon acquired an aura of mystery because of their secret organization methods, which awoke a profound echo in the religious spirit of the peasant masses. Using symbols to transmit their messages, spreading their propaganda through the ballads sung by peasant folk singers from fair to fair, creating martyrs in a land where a people with no present and no destiny were ripe for a message that would bring some meaning into their lives, the League movement led the peasant masses of the Northeast to achieve, in a surprisingly short time, the evolution that had taken so many decades in other parts of the country.

In order to understand the unprecedented phenomenon of the formation of class-consciousness among the peasants of the sugar zone in little more than five years, we must take into account the tenacity with which the landowning class clung to its constellation of feudal privileges, in a desperate attempt to save them. On the great sugar plantation, as we have seen, public and private authority was one and the same thing. The laborer had no concept of a public power except through the police force occasionally called in by the landowner to solve some serious problem. The daily defense of property against possible incursions was carried out by the private police, who were more or less out in the open. In this way, the peasant did not clearly realize where the arbitration of the landowner ended and the action of the public power began. When he became aware of the conflict of interests between himself and the landowner, he also came to feel open hostility for the public power. The state was nothing but the higher instrument of oppression used by the landowning class. Thus, when the League movement started, the only leaders who managed to succeed were those who spoke out openly against the public power, symbol of the complex of interests represented by the landowning class. In this way, from the very beginning, the possibility of a paternalistic type of leadership, based on a distribution of favors paid for out of the public coffers, was eliminated.

Up to 1962, the organization of the peasant class of the

sugar plantations showed all the characteristics of the classic type of revolutionary regimentation. The leaders, whether Marxist or Catholic, all insisted on saying aloud that they were fighting against the existing order of things. They took off from the principle that the existing socioeconomic organization was unjust. The peasants organized themselves not only to protest, but also to demand that the existing order be changed. Since they were not entitled to any "rights," the simple fact that they were organizing meetings was considered by the landowning class to be an act of sedition, warranting suppression by violent means. In this way, a potential leader of the peasant masses had to be prepared to meet violence, which would be possible only with the help of other forms of violence. To strengthen his positions, any and every leader found himself compelled to speak a revolutionary language, although he was not called upon to establish definite revolutionary objectives in the social sphere. We must admit that the irreducible revolutionary content, common to all leaders of the peasant movement in the sugar zone, was limited to the intention of removing the prevailing feudal structure, and this seemed to call for a mobilization of violence. Their implicit objective was to extend to the cane workers the rights that had been granted to urban workers many years before.

The passing of the Rural Workers' Statute [4] by congress at the beginning of 1963 had profound effects on the Peasant League movement. When this law was passed (and perhaps it was for this very reason that it did manage to get through congress), the general opinion was that it would take many years for the legislation to be effectively carried out. The implementing regulations would require detailed studies of the characteristics of each rural area, and this would open the way for all kinds of procrastination.

We need only consider what still happens in the attempts to carry out the provisions of the "Minimal Wage" law in the Northeastern urban centers. There has been a minimum of pressure to comply with the provisions laid down by this law in view of the enormous surplus in manpower. Many factories, particularly those situated in the smaller cities, operate a shift system, paying wages below the legal minimum. The alternative that the factory owner offers the workers is the closing down of the supplementary shifts, which lessens pressure on the part of the workers to achieve enforcement of the law.

Since surplus labor on the land is even greater, it was easy to predict the future of a law extending to rural workers the guarantee of a minimal wage fixed by the public power, together with certain other social favors. However, these considerations did not take into account the new reality of the sugar zone, where powerful semi-clandestine organizations had sprung up, all of them infected with genuine revolutionary fervor and with their objectives not yet clearly defined. Under the protection of the new law, these organizations suddenly came to the fore, cloaked in the legal mantle of rural trade unions, which permitted the peasant class of the sugar zone to take prompt action with extraordinary effect. What for many had seemed but a distant aspiration, became in a surprisingly short time an immediate objective. Thus, in one year, the sugar workers managed to achieve objectives that for decades had remained moribund for a large section of the urban proletariat, who had only achieved these benefits through paternalistic concession.

The spectacular victory of the cane workers, leading in record time to the enforcement of a law that not only substantially increased their real wages, but also altered the basis of their secular working conditions, was facilitated by the concomitant action of other economic factors. We have previously seen that the landowning class of the Northeast had been trying to keep wages down in order to retain its share of the national market. If wages went up, as they did after 1963, Northeastern industry would obviously no longer be in a position to defend its quota in the southern market. However, after 1960, important changes had taken place in the world sugar market as a result of the Cuban Revolution. Once Cuba had been eliminated from competition for the United States market in 1961, new prospects opened up for Brazilian sugar in a protective and highly priced market. The progressive elimination of the quota system in the American market after 1962, coincided with a sharp rise in world sugar prices, caused by the reduction of Cuban output. The lengthy period during which exports had been supported by subsidies paid for by the Brazilian consumer was succeeded by a period of rising international prices, higher than those prevailing in the home market. In order to avoid an excessive rise in domestic prices and, at the same time, to defend the sugar industry from sudden fluctuations in the overseas market, the federal government devised an export tax which would permit the formation of a fund for reequipping the sugar industry, particularly in the Northeast.

In view of the altered circumstances, the Northeastern sugar industry began to export its total surplus, abandoning all concern with the country's southern market. The social pressure for a rise in wages ceased to be dangerous and began to be regarded with complacency, since it became a powerful argument for justifying both the demand for elimination of the export tax, and the rise of domestic prices to the international level. The fear that a rise in the relative domestic prices of sugar would create unsalable surpluses was replaced by the desire for exportable surpluses. Even more important, since domestic prices were lower than export prices, a common bond was forged between the interests of estate owners and workers. By exerting pressure for a rise in wages, the workers provided the owners with arguments to justify a rise in prices in the direct interest of the estate owners, whose profits increase as the price of the product increases.

The period of great victories for the peasant organizations of the sugar zone, which lasted from 1962 to 1963, is also the period when their revolutionary potential begins to decline. We have already pointed out that the revolutionary character of these organizations was less in their objectives —never clearly defined by the leaders or in the consciousness of the peasants, but existing merely as a revolt against the landowning class and its repressive force, the public power —than in the methods they were obliged to use in order to survive in the face of violence. Had it not been for the special circumstances that arose in the sugar market, the movement might have developed in a very different way. If pressure against a rise in real wages, exerted by an alienated feudal class, had continued for some time, social tensions in the Northeastern sugar complex would very possibly have erupted into violence. However, thanks chiefly to the changes brought about in the world sugar market by the Cuban Revolution, circumstances arose that altered the course of events. The powerful social forces that had been concentrated to break down the barrier of the feudal structure were channelled into legally defined objectives to be achieved without compromising the bases of the social structure, the old feudal landowning class taking over the function of directing the new capitalist order. Nevertheless, this clear definition of objectives, able to function as the catalyst for powerful social forces in revolutionary gestation, was only possible without an open clash of interests with the landowning class, because of the special circumstances.

What consequences for the future can we infer from the changes that have so recently taken place in the Northeastern sugar economy? In the first place, there seems to be no doubt that the foundations of the old feudal regime, which has persisted over the centuries, have definitely been completely undermined. There has been a switch, almost abruptly, to a paid labor regime of an advanced type, that is, a regime based on collective working contracts in which the working class is clearly conscious of its interests, and there is an advanced pattern of organized labor. On the other hand, we must recognize that the most important group of Northeastern peasants has become a privileged sector in terms of the peasant class as a whole. With their wages on a par with those of urban workers, and equipped by their advanced organization to carry out all the advantages of social legislation, the peasants of the sugar zone will, within a few years, have been transformed into a genuine rural middle class. A legally established money wage, with the social advantages it offers, places them well above the typical sharecropper, artisan, or even smallholder. The social movements in which they may participate will always be directed toward clearly defined objectives and closely bound up with their own interests, all of them translatable into the legal language of contracts. Taking into account the existence of a great surplus of manpower throughout the rural areas, the worker protected by a collective contract is soon led to demarcate the limits of his own interests, aware that he forms part of a privileged minority.

It would, however, be oversimplifying to say that we are simply dealing with a process in which the revolutionary potential has been exhausted. Is the sugar economy in a condition to provide a solid basis for the numerous class of workers who have suddenly benefited from all the advantages of a relatively progressive social legislation? Or has a high cost economy been created which survives only because of temporary special circumstances? We have already seen that the recent changes have closed the country's southern markets to Northeastern output. Thus we have gone back to the period before 1930 when the Northeast depended on the overseas market for placing its considerable surplus production. We have, therefore, also gone back to subjection to all the vicissitudes caused by the fluctuations and uncertainties of the overseas market for tropical products. We must stress the fact that the reentry of the Northeast into the world sugar market was not the result of an effective improvement in the competitive power of its product, but the result of the relative disorganization of this market caused by factors whose full implications are as yet unknown. The Northeastern sugar economy continues to have the lowest productivity of all the world's sugar exporting regions. Agricultural yield per hectare is extremely low. And the productivity of the human factor employed in the agricultural sector is even lower. It was precisely these adverse productivity conditions that in the past prevented the Northeast from competing in the international market, and necessitated the quota system to insure its participation in the southern domestic market. Given the substantial rise in costs caused by the recent changes, it can be assumed that the Northeast will only stay in the overseas markets as long as the abnormal conditions of the recent past continue to exist. We must expect supply to return to its former level, either through the recovery of Cuban harvests or through increased output by other areas as the result of a relatively high price level. Although price levels should remain considerably higher than the averages of the three decades preceding the Cuban Revolution, there is only a remote possibility that these prices will remain high enough to shelter, for any length of time, the extremely low level of current Northeastern productivity.

If we take into account the multiple factors affecting the problem as a whole, we must realize that the situation recently created in the Northeastern sugar economy is basically unstable. The domestic market, with its regular growth at controlled prices, has been left to the more capitalized and more efficient industry of the South. Any significant decrease in the foreign market will entail grave consequences for the Northeastern sugar crop, which will have to be purchased for stockholding, or will require subsidies for exporting. This would lead to the need for a policy of controlling production similar to that of the 1930's, only concentrated in the Northeast, whose output would otherwise find itself partially without a market. It will no longer prove possible, however, to cut down on production as in the past, since costs have become much more rigid as the result of social compromises. In order to alter the tendencies that have emerged, the elements responsible for sugar production must start making an extraordinary effort to increase productivity. Proper irrigation and land drainage, introduction of advanced fertilizer techniques, and an adequate combination of cane varieties are all called for, but these are not short-term undertakings in view of the lack of basic studies on soil resources and water supplies in the region. Cane cutting and transportation techniques, a better combination of the factors involved in operating economic-sized milling units, in fact, the whole structure of the economy, would have to be renewed. Most of the present suppliers would have to disappear and the number of "usinas" would have to be substantially reduced, if the industry hopes to reach levels of productivity comparable to those of its competitors in world markets.

However, the effort needed to bring the industry up-to-date technically and to increase productivity, will encounter the large obstacle of an enormous surplus in manpower protected by powerful trade unions. A consistent policy designed to raise productivity will necessarily create widespread unemployment, since the present labor surplus is estimated at about half the population now permanently employed, even if we do not take into account the introduction of up-to-date techniques of cane cutting. Part of this labor force can, at least in the initial stages, be employed in work arising out of the actual investment plan to increase productivity. Nevertheless, the social problem to be faced is enormous, all the more so since the conquests by the working class are so recent.

If we were to attempt to sum up the present situation in the Northeastern sugar economy, we would say that the special conditions that led to the elimination of feudal ties have given the economy a premature rigidity. This will make it more difficult to effect the transition toward a capitalist structure that is sufficiently flexible to adapt itself to the contingencies of the foreign market.

By unduly prolonging its defense of the feudal structure, the landowning class missed the best opportunity for laying the foundations of a viable capitalist economy, that is, the period when it was still easy to cut down on costs and when social resistance was nil. A similar evolution, at a much more advanced stage, occurred with our railroad industry: the opportunity to modernize at a time when the road system was just beginning to get under way, and salaries could still be cut without too much difficulty, was thrown away. Once this opportunity had been lost, there was no alternative but to hand over to the government obsolete structures and deficits that threatened to grow exponentially.

There is no doubt that the development of the Northeastern sugar economy over the next few years is directly dependent on the actions of the landowning class. The peasant movement has already defined itself, in its basic lines, as a process for consolidating the status of a wage-earning class and for defending contractual benefits. It remains to be seen whether the present landowning class, marked with all the vices of the feudal structure which it has not yet discarded, can create the conditions needed for survival of the agricultural industry, or whether it will have to abandon it as so much scrap iron or a machine for creating public deficits.[5]

The Intermediate Zone

The humid coastal lowlands, originally covered with tropical forests and hence known as the Mata zone,[6] occupy only a fraction of Northeastern territory. Strictly speaking, the zone extends only from the State of Bahia to the State of Pernambuco. In Paraíba and Rio Grande do Norte, it appears at intervals in a few valleys and then reappears in Maranhão outside the geographical boundaries of the Northeast. The largest area of Northeastern territory is covered by the Caatinga zone. The word means "white forest," and gives a graphic idea of the Indians' vision of the sparse and transparent vegetation that covers this immense region during the long dry season.[7] Within the extensive Caatinga zone, there are certain areas where special characteristics of the soil and the elevation, by permitting greater precipitation and retention of moisture, create marked climatic differences. These subregions are particularly important in the state of Ceará, where they play a role similar to that of the Mata zone in concentrating the population, and in the states of Alagoas, Pernambuco and Paraíba, where they assume the characteristics of an intermediate zone between the Mata and the Caatinga.

The transition zone between the Mata and the Caatinga is generally known as the Agreste, being distinguished from the Sertão proper by a higher degree of moisture and by the generally better quality of the soil.[8] The degree of moisture is insufficient for sugar cultivation, but permits the cultivation of cereals in more stable conditions than those in the extensive Sertão region.[9]

Original settlement of the Agreste region, like that of the Sertão as a whole, was owing to the need to provide cattle for the sugar economy. The regions were penetrated and allotments of land were demanded, which allowed the whole of the Caatinga zone to be appropriated by landowners from colonial times onwards. This prior appropriation of extensive lands that were only effectually occupied economically at a much later date, marked the evolution of the Caatinga economy both in the Agreste and in the Sertão. The sugar economy had grown up, not around the land, but around a substantial capital. This capital, concentrated in equipment, buildings, and slaves, was the nucleus around which the whole economy revolved. Land was appropriated as the capacity to produce sugar expanded. The rural community was formed within the large plantation under the authority of the owner of the capital, who by extension also owned the land. In the Caatinga economy, capital consisted of cattle herds, whose physical growth was dependent on the availability of land and water. Landownership was what insured the possibility of stock rearing. The Caatinga community was formed under the authority of the landowner. The man who inhabited another's land, even if he did not work for the other man, was bound to him as to a person invested with authority.

The Agreste region was settled by the surplus population of the Mata zone during the long decline of the sugar economy. In colonial times, runaway Negroes, such as those who founded the Palmares Republic in the seventeenth century, had settled in the region and established a subsistence economy. This process of population transfer was intensified by the abolition of slavery, causing a considerable demographic concentration in the Agreste zone. This can be explained by the fact that only in this region (or in similar regions, such as the Serras in Ceará) did man find it possible to survive on a subsistence economy. In effect, a man could only remain in the Mata zone if he were tied to the sugar economy; every time sugar production stagnated, which occurred for lengthy and repeated periods, the surplus population tended to abandon the great estates. In the Sertão, a man could only survive by taking part in the cattle economy, whose limited demand for manpower was even further curtailed by the stagnation of its chief market, the sugar economy. Climatic conditions in the Sertão did not allow a man to settle down on the basis of a purely subsistence agriculture. Hence, the population that could not find employment on the sugar or cattle estates started moving into the Agreste, and managed to survive until urban development began to attract a steady flow of emigration from the Northeast.

Another factor that conditioned the economic evolution of the Agreste was the introduction of bush cotton in early colonial times. Since it is an annual crop, bush cotton can be produced by means similar to those used for subsistence crops, i.e., within a family unit and with little or no specialized agricultural technique. Both in the domestic and in the foreign markets, cotton became a source of money income for the peasant mass who settled in the Agreste, long before an economic use was found for their surplus food production.

Let us now see how these factors have evolved and given rise to the type of economy that now exists in the Agreste. The basic element, which conditioned the evolution of all the others, was the prior appropriation of land by individuals interested in stock-raising. Thus, before any process of capitalization took place, the land was appropriated in the form of large estates. As we have already observed, this phenomenon is common both to the Agreste and to the Sertão. However, in view of the topographical characteristics of the Agreste, and the superior quality of much of its land, estates in the Agreste were generally smaller. Some of the estates were, in the course of centuries, divided by inheritance, giving rise to a regime of small estates which in some places can even be described as small holdings. However, this phenomenon was an exception, and accounted for little more than one-tenth of the land in the Agreste. The greater part of the land continues in the hands of great landowners, who are, for the most part, absentees. The evolution of these great estates was entirely based on stock-raising because of a curious association with subsistence forms of agriculture. The surplus population that flowed into the Agreste was given permission to work the soil within the boundaries of a great estate, on condition that the land would be abandoned whenever the owner needed it to graze his cattle.

Sometimes the landowner was simply interested in the clearance of the Caatinga, carried out by the settlers before planting subsistence crops or cotton; once cleared, the Caatinga became a natural pasture which could be taken over as the herds increased. The worker was always given the opportunity to move to another part of the Caatinga and start all over again the endless task of clearing lands for pasture. At other times, the landowner was less interested in the possibilities of natural pasturelands for the future than in the stubble provided by the settler's crops. After the harvest, the settler handed over his fields for the owner's cattle to graze in, at a time when pastures were at their poorest because of the dry season. These combinations developed as the population grew, and made the land increasingly costly for the settler who worked it. After a certain period, the landowner only allowed the workers to cultivate the soil in return for the stubble fodder in those exceptional cases where the land was poor, and, in the majority of cases, demanded a share of cotton production as rent. In other cases, the landowner demanded one or two days of free labor weekly as compensation for the use of his land.

The growth of the population on the one hand, and the valorization of the cattle industry on the other, placed the agricultural workers of the Agreste in an increasingly precarious situation. As the family agricultural unit was simply a complement to the stock-rearing activities of the great estate, there was no possibility for organizing agriculture on a basis of increased capitalization. The small cultivator, attached to the great estate, was only provided with the amount of land that employed his family at the most primitive technical level. To increase his income, he would have needed to use more up-to-date methods of cultivation, which would require much more capital and land than that available to him. Would these changes operate in the interests of the landowner? Would not the credit needed to raise the standards of farming methods create a greater bond between the cultivator and the land that its owner wanted to have free for his cattle each year? We must remember that improved agricultural techniques would necessarily increase the cultivator's income, but would not increase the rent reverting to the landowner for the use of his land. On the other hand, improvements in agricultural techniques could not be carried out without greatly reducing the number of workers attached to the estate. Direct knowledge of the region indicates that the number of agricultural workers would not be decreased by less than three-quarters, if the Agreste cultivator were to be given an adequate income. It is obvious that a decrease in the number of workers, and an increase in their incomes, would have to result in a rise in the cost of the manpower employed by the landowner in stock-rearing and other activities. Thus, there is a conflict of interests between the mass of cultivators who work the land for themselves, and the owner of this land.

The workers who live off the agriculture that is complementary to the cattle industry generally do not live within the estates, or if they do, they are attached to the estate in communities, as a result of the long-standing obligation to hand over the land for pasture every year. This fact proved highly significant in the recent evolution of social movements in the Agreste. Since they lived in communities, the people of this region were in a better position to become aware of their common problems than were those of the Mata zone. This explains not only why the Peasant League movement sprang up on the Agreste borders, but also why it spread so rapidly through the region. Living, as a rule, outside the boundaries of the great estate, the workers of the Agreste were much more accessible to any form of regimentation at a time when the great landowners were trying, at all costs, to isolate their tenants from any outside influence. For this reason, it was in the small communities of the Agreste that Peasant League centers were openly established, whereas in the estates of the Mata zone they existed as secret societies.

The struggle of the Agreste peasants was from the very beginning directed toward defending possession of the land they cultivated. Pressure for the permanent occupation of more and more land, from both the cane plantations along the border zone between the Agreste and the Mata and the cattle estates of the Agreste, was acting as a force for expelling a growing section of the Agreste population from the land which it had settled. Unlike the cane worker, who merely sells his labor and struggles for wages, the Agreste cultivator, even if he lives within an estate, is conscious of his bond with the land that he cultivates. This bond sows the seeds for the belief common to all peasants, that even if they are not entitled to ownership of the land, they are a least entitled to possession. It was the defense of this virtual right, formulated as a demand for indemnity for a peasant forced to abandon the land he had long cultivated, that led to the pooling of effort in the early stages of the League movement. But mere preservation of the right to possession of the land would have been meaningless, if the rent paid to the landowner continued to rise inexorably. And, as we have seen, this was the natural tendency in view of the population increase and valorization of the stock-herding industry. At this point, the victories won by the cane workers had important repercussions in the Agreste. Once the wages of rural workers had been increased, it was obvious that the rent paid to the landowner in the days of "subjection" was a preposterous form of exploiting the worker. It was estimated that, in this way, within one or two years the worker paid rent equal to the total value of his land. Nevertheless, elimination of payments in the form of free labor does not prevent the rent from being increased. Furthermore, under the present condition of extremely low agricultural productivity, whatever the rent, the worker is in no position to pay it without reducing his standard of living well below the standard permitted by the minimum wage. And for this reason it is probable that the social problem of the Agreste will develop in a different way than that in the Mata zone.

Despite their low living standards, a large proportion of Agreste workers do not earn enough to live by their work in the region. They supplement their incomes by seasonal emigration to the Mata zone, where they work as cane cutters, which is possible because the cane cutting season partly coincides with the dead season in the Agreste, or at least with the cotton picking season, an activity that can be left to the women and children. Given the changes that are occurring in the sugar economy, a decrease in the demand for manpower from the Agreste is predictable, with a more effective utilization of the labor force bound by contract in the Mata zone. If this possibility of supplementary income, open to the more needy workers of the Agreste, is reduced or remains static, we can expect the rent burden to become correspondingly heavy for these workers. Now, present conditions of productivity being what they are, even if rent were totally eliminated, the bulk of workers in the Agreste would still be unable to achieve a standard of living comparable to the standard permitted by the minimum wage. And since the cane workers have already achieved this standard, it is probable that the Agreste workers will fight to attain a similar one, with the complete abolition of all rent paid to the landowners as their immediate objective.

If we were to try to summarize current tendencies, we would say that in order to meet the demands of the workers for a rapid improvement in their living conditions, it would be necessary to reorganize the existing structure of agriculture in the Agreste, with a view to increasing productivity. This would require an increase in the amount of land per family and capitalization at a much higher level than the present one. This reorganization conflicts with the interests of the landowners, and is not viable from the peasants' point of view, since their struggle is directed toward defending their possession of the land. By defending their possession, the peasants are indirectly defending the present organization of the agricultural economy, with its large manpower surplus that makes it impossible to increase the productivity of their work. To raise the standard of farming methods for a family entitled to a mere five hectares of land, when they would actually need at least twenty, is not a feat that can be economically accomplished. In the present structure, any land rent whatsoever is exorbitant insofar as it depresses the workers' living standards below adequate subsistence levels.

By defending possession of the land, the peasants are, in fact, demanding the complete abolition of land rent, which amounts to the same thing as demanding ownership of the land. The terms in which social struggle in the Agreste is now being couched will therefore inevitably lead to a definition of positions that can only be resolved by means of radical processes. As the simple division of the land would create serious losses for the major economic industry, which is stock-rearing, besides perpetuating the small-holding system, it is only natural that landowners should oppose any such agrarian reform. They would consider it to be completely irrational, and not simply to affect their own interests. For the workers, however, who are fighting for minimum living standards, the objectives are no more irrational than is the present situation, in which the landowners, protected by their privileges, are able to prevent improvements in the technical standards of agriculture in order to serve their interests. The landowners can now enforce an increase in land rents, while the workers, who must occupy poorer and poorer lands, are obliged to cope with declining productivity.

The Sertão Caatinga

The Sertão is the only area in the Northeast that can be classified as semi-arid. Rainfall in the Sertão differs from that of the Mata and Agreste zones. The latter zones benefit from rainfall from the sea that occurs in winter, whereas the Sertão has summer rainfall, which comes from fronts moving from Maranhão or the south. This pattern of rainfall is responsible for the phenomenon of the droughts. With the exception of the "Serras," [10] precipitation throughout the Sertão region is much lower than in the Agreste. The area with the lowest precipitation is a strip extending from northern Bahia to Rio Grande do Norte, passing through the interior of Pernambuco and Paraíba immediately beyond the Agreste zone. This strip acts as a kind of division between the rains coming from the eastern Atlantic and those that develop from continental fronts, producing an average rainfall of less than 24 inches, when for the Sertão region as a whole the average is not less than 800 millimeters or 31½ inches. The semi-arid nature of the Sertão region is caused by a peculiar combination of the region's hydrological and geological characteristics. Average rainfall is not different from that of other areas that have a favorable climate for agriculture.

However, the underlying rocks hold very little moisture owing to the lack of sedimentary beds, which leaves the surface water subject to a high rate of evaporation. Because the rains tend to come in violent downpours, the sedimentary formations have been heavily eroded, and the crystalline rock has a very thin soil covering throughout the region. Where the sedimentary layer was very deep and could not easily be washed away, as was the case with large areas in Piauí or the Tucano basin in Bahia, a process of leaching has occurred, with vertical drainage of the most important constituent elements of the soil. In these regions, the Caatinga is even more scanty than in the typical areas of crystalline rock.

The natural vegetation of the region became adapted to these conditions by a process of xerophytism, which finds its ultimate expression in the Caatinga as a particular type of tropical forest. For eight months of the year, in order to survive, the Caatinga's vital activities almost stop, and it becomes a phantom forest. During this lethargic period, the plants live on reserves of water stored in their roots, a reserve that enables them to recover surprisingly as soon as the rainy season approaches. The approaching rains may last only a very short while, and the plant prepares to store this new moisture like a hunter stalking an elusive prey. For this reason, the xerophytic vegetation uses its reserves intensively as soon as the rains begin to approach, producing the marvellous spectacle of the sudden transformation of the Caatinga into a green forest.

The phenomenon of periodic droughts is caused by disturbances in precipitation. For reasons which still await the explanation that might be provided by more detailed meteorological studies, there occurs a failure in precipitation that, in extreme cases, can be as high as 30 percent for the whole of the semi-arid region. The disturbance, however, is not limited to a reduction in the amount of rain that falls. It also takes the form of a greater concentration and irregularity in the rainfall, which causes a reduction of the already limited quantity of moisture retained by the soil for use by the vegetation or by animal life. In short, less water falls, and the amount retained is even scantier. The Caatinga is designed to resist the drought, even if it lasts as long as two or three years, which sometimes happens. Xerophytism, in fact, is a process by which the vegetation adapts itself to these climatic contingencies.

Occupation of the Sertão Caatinga was, by and large, carried out in a form similar to that of the Agreste. The search for land and water for the cattle industry led man to explore the whole of the Caatinga, going as far as the borders of the moist tropical forest that stretches along Maranhão, south of Piauí and north of Goiás. Penetration led to appropriation of unused lands granted by allotment and establishment of cattle ranches in places where the water supply was most reliable. Subsequent evolution took place within the framework of these immense cattle estates.

For a long time the only kind of organized economy in the Sertão Caatinga was extensive stock-raising. In this region, as a rule, ten hectares of land are required to support each head of cattle. In addition, the cattle must move about during the dry season, since the regular water holes are limited and are almost always situated in the higher regions. These adverse conditions called for a painful adaptation by the species introduced into the region, so that the predominant strain has a stronger bone structure, longer legs for roaming through the thorny scrub, and is extremely lean-fleshed. Stock-rearing

absorbs a small proportion of manpower, and its growth was limited by the availability of permanent water holes and the ever increasing distances at which these were found. The impact of the droughts—there is at least one severe drought per decade—was disastrous to the livestock, since the drying up of the water holes not only made it difficult for the herds to survive in the Caatinga, but made their removal to the permanent water holes a hazardous undertaking, with thousands of cattle dying on the way in a sacrifice that amounted to a virtual hecatomb. In this way, the Sertão herds had increased and been decimated in cycles that were repeated from colonial times to the beginning of this century. Nevertheless, during the long period in which the Sertão was almost exclusively a stock-breeding region, the drought problem had limited social effect for, since the human population was very scanty and there was an abundant supply of cattle for slaughtering, man's survival was never threatened.

It was in the nineteenth century that the growth of cotton acquired significance in the Sertão region. An arborescent variety, native to the region, began to be increasingly cultivated in large areas of the Caatinga. Crossbreeding with other varieties enabled cotton cultivation to increase. It is important to stress that the original Caatinga variety, known as "moco," is a xerophytic plant, and is therefore adapted to survive in the peculiar conditions of its natural environment. In the second half of the last century, particularly during the 'sixties, with the occurrence of the great "cotton hunger" caused by the Civil War in the United States, interest in Sertão cotton grew and cotton cultivation became firmly rooted.

The consequences of the growth of cotton cultivation were of great significance for the Sertão. By creating the conditions for the absorption of an increasing amount of manpower, cotton cultivation provided an outlet for the people who had previously gone to the Agreste to establish a subsistence economy, and who could now move to the Sertão

where they could find permanent employment. In this way, the great cattle estate evolved in the direction of a mixed economy. Cotton not only created a source of money income for the landowner, but provided seed, which in the form of cottonseed cake is an excellent source of protein for cattle. On the other hand, the labor force working on cotton had to plant food crops or "vegetables" (the name given by the Backlander to all the food crops he cultivates) for its own consumption. After harvesting, the stubble from the food crops could be used as cattle feed, which also benefited the owner of the cattle ranch.

This apparently happy combination of stock-breeding and the cultivation of tree cotton changed the basis of the Sertão economy, and transformed the droughts into a social problem of considerable dimensions. The settlers who flocked to the Sertão to seek the advantages offered by cotton cultivation and the abundance of food crops produced during "good" winters,[11] were really being attracted by a fiendish trap. The worker who settled on one of the great estates in the Sertão was obliged to plant cotton on a sharecropping basis. The owner financed the plantation of the crop by advancing seeds and the capital needed to defray production expenses. Even today, it is usual for an estate owner to raise money from a government bank and use it for financing the settlers who work with him on a sharecropping basis.

This financial backing is repaid, measured in bales of cotton, with concealed interest at a rate not less than the rates charged by the usual intermediaries, that is to say, at about five times the official bank rate. In addition to the interest charged for his financial outlay, the estate owner is, as a rule, entitled to half the output. If the worker has not been financed in this way, he is usually obliged to sell his entire yield beforehand, "on the tree," at prices fixed to suit the buyer. However, these are still not the aspects that have the most negative effect on the worker's life.

Tree cotton, since it grows in the adverse conditions of the

Caatinga, gives an extremely low yield per hectare. Although the tree variety does not have to be replanted annually like the bush cotton of the Agreste, and therefore does not require as much effort on the part of the Sertão cotton-grower, the latter has to cope with lower yields, which gives him a much smaller income than that of his Agreste counterpart. This income is in no way sufficient to allow him to survive, unless he can count on free housing and food. Cotton-growing must therefore be supported by a subsistence economy if the Sertão settler is to survive. In this way, by settling on a great estate in the Sertão, the worker has assumed all the risks involved in maintaining a subsistence economy in the semi-arid Caatinga.

The production of food crops is carried out within the great estate by individual settlers, the lower lands that hold moisture for longer periods being put aside for this purpose. When these lands are of good quality, the estate owner usually demands a half or one-third of the output, but this only occurs in exceptional cases. During a drought, losses in cotton production are limited, but in most cases food crops are affected and there is a total crop failure. The worker who does not make enough out of cotton to survive is then left totally destitute, and is forced to emigrate in order to escape starvation. In this way, since the 'sixties of the last century, the droughts have ceased to be calamities that decimated the cattle population, and have become genuine social catastrophes.

With the drought problem assuming the proportions of a national calamity, the federal government began to concern itself with the problem directly. From the beginning of this century, special organizations were set up whose specific function it was to "fight the droughts"; [12] considerable sums were devoted to this end, albeit in an intermittent fashion. However, the men who demanded government action had a distorted view of the problem because their own interests were at stake. These were the owners of the great estates, who measured the losses caused by the droughts in terms of losses in livestock. In effect, the efforts of federal government technicians only achieved continuity, and proved effective when it was directed toward a solution of the problems of the stock-breeding industry. Medium sized and small dams were constructed in thousands, making it possible for water to be stored on nearly all the estates of any considerable size, and this gave greater stability to the stock-rearing industry. Roads were built in all directions, facilitating the use of trucks for transporting the cattle to cooler regions during the more rigorous summers. In brief, the effects of the droughts on livestock were considerably mitigated. However, the construction of larger dams that were intended to provide important irrigation schemes to help stabilize the food supply during periods of drought has never gone beyond the stage of building simple reservoirs. Government appropriation of land for irrigation could never be effectively carried out, and when irrigation works were started, they were generally on the lands of the great estate owners. Instead of concerning themselves with the problem of providing food for the populace during periods of drought, the estate owners have begun to grow crops with some commercial interest, such as sugarcane for the production of cane spirits.

Thus, the extraordinary effort to try to solve the drought problem made by the federal government during the last half century has been deflected from its true social objective, and has become an instrument for consolidating the great cattle estates, whose basis had been threatened by the social calamities of the droughts. No concerted effort was made to help the immense mass of workers who live by sharecropping to cope with the droughts. The estate owners began to demand that the government provide real or fictitious employment for the population during the crisis periods, near their usual working places, in order to avoid dispersion of the labor force. In this way, too, the government has protected the estate owners, who maintained their structural manpower surplus and continued to exploit an extremely cheap labor force employed in antisocial agriculture. In this way, the Sertão Caatinga has managed to achieve a surprising density of population, if we consider the low standards of technique that continue to prevail in the region and the poverty of natural resources. The Jaguaribe Valley—which has been called "the largest dry river in the world"—with an area of about 80,000 square kilometers, supports a population of more than 20 persons per square kilometer, a figure unparalleled for any comparable area.

The workers of the Sertão Caatinga, like those of the Agreste, generally live in clusters that in most cases are situated within the boundaries of a great estate. As they are not under pressure to quit the lands where they work, and have been led to believe that the roots of their problem lie in the rigors of nature, these workers are in a much less favorable position for becoming aware of their situation, or for entertaining any thoughts of changing it by their own actions. The social problem of the Sertão is owing to the excess of population that continues to accumulate in the region, drawn by the promise of a food supply that is really totally unstable. Nevertheless, because of the very fact that the people live in neighborly communities, the social tensions of the other areas, particularly those of the Agreste, have repercussions on these communities. The victories that the peasants have gained in the last decade in the latter zone, which have led to a reduction of land rent, will certainly have an impact on the Sertão area. The present agricultural economy of the Sertão, independent of the landowning system, cannot survive without undergoing drastic changes. Its low level of productivity and the vulnerability of food production are incompatible with the present density of its population, and any social movement that might arise in the area will, of necessity, have a marked revolutionary bias. Whenever an economic structure does not permit the workers' interests to be reconciled with those of development, social movements take the form of revolutionary processes and exert pressure toward supersedure of the structure. In the Sertão, simple elimination of land rent will not provide a solution for the situation of the great majority of agricultural workers. An effort is needed to reorganize the whole agricultural economy, with a view to eliminating the numerous defects introduced into this economy by one of the most irrational forms of estate ownership that has ever existed anywhere—so that the working masses can be provided with adequate living conditions.

Conclusions

If we consider the agriculture of the Northeast as a whole, we must conclude that the constant factor in its recent evolution has been a strange paradox. Increased production has coincided with a greater irrationality in the economic system, analyzed from the point of view of the interests of the working community directly involved.

Thus, in the Mata zone, expansion of the cane fields has brought even greater misery to the workers, depriving them of the possibility of producing their own food requirements. In the Agreste, valorization of the stock-rearing industry has created pressure for a rise in the land rent paid by a worker whose productivity is stationary or declining. In the Sertão, improved conditions for expanding the cattle industry, created by the efforts of the government, and increased cotton production with the aid of official financing, have allowed the population to increase, which requires a corresponding growth in food production on lands that are increasingly subject to climatic irregularities. We are, therefore, faced with an economy that, by its growth, aggravates its structural problems. We have seen that a partial solution for these problems was found in the Mata zone, thanks to a providential rise in the overseas prices of the product, which justified a similar rise in the home market. And we have also seen that this solution created new potential problems that could challenge the survival of the agricultural sugar industry in its present form, with no prospect of an economically viable alternative organization for the industry. In the Agreste, problems are so bad that a rational solution within the present structural context has already become impractical. In the Sertão, although the problems are still in an incipient stage because they have not yet been clearly formulated in the consciousness of the masses, everything indicates that, once social forces have been unleashed, an even greater impasse will occur than that now existing in the Agreste. From the point of view of the region as a whole, food production has been diverted from the moist areas to the semi-arid zones. In this way, the urban population is becoming increasingly dependent on surplus food grown in areas subject to the phenomena of droughts, and this has grave consequences for the nascent industrial development.

Whenever economic development unleashes forces that operate in an antisocial direction, we can be certain that we are faced with a process that is not evolutionary, but revolutionary. A society may remain stationary for thousands of years, but from the moment its productive forces begin to grow, it will be obliged to find some way of reconciling the interests of groups that play dynamic roles in the productive process. If the structural framework operates in a perverse way, degrading the situation of the workers while it increases production, we may take for granted that there will be a rupture of this system, unless some "miracle" occurs, as it did recently for the sugar economy.

The unwonted slowness with which the peasant classes in the Northeast became aware of their problems can be explained by taking into account the rudimentary nature of community life confined within the great estates. Whether they were dispersed, as in the Mata zone, or occasionally gathered together in communities, as in the Agreste and the Sertão, the peasants were, until recently, completely immersed in the social reality of the estate.

The only authority recognized was that of the "Colonel" [13] and his accomplices, who served the state authorities merely to give formal legality to his own wishes. "Political" activity was thought of as a tournament in which the competition for preeminence was among leaders of local groups, who were nearly always great landowners or their surrogates. Control of positions of authority also implied easier access to the favors of the federal government, which were translated as works of direct interest to the great estates. Political activity engaged only a small minority of the population conscious of the benefits they could reap from it. The worker's family, requiring the labor of all children over the age of eight, was denied the opportunity of literacy, and this also eliminated any possibility of rising to the state of effective citizenship. The great mass of the workers, therefore, constituted a kind of sub-citizenry, closer to the former slaves than to the civil population, since its participation in social life was limited almost exclusively to supplying the labor force. This situation is, however, changing with increasing speed. One important factor operating in this direction has been the anxiety to multiply municipal governments as a means of participating in the federal tax collection.[14] Legal limitations to the creation of new municipalities are openly mocked at, with new municipal governments coming into being for communities consisting of only a few hundred people. These local governments provide the impulse for rudimentary forms of urban life, since they spend what they receive from the federal government in creating public services and supporting an incipient bureaucracy. The existence of commercial and bureaucratic activities in these villages has stimulated the start of a social life that acts as a corrosive force on the prestige of the former political leaders. The horizon of preoccupations is widening and politics are taking a new turn, making it increasingly difficult to control the electorate. Processes of acquiring literacy are also being simplified, thus creating an increasingly heterogeneous body of electors. In short, the old power structure has been challenged, making room for political opportunists of several types. These manage to get themselves elected on the basis of all sorts of promises, vying with each other to excite the imagination of the masses, creating the expectation of growing improvements, and inducing the former settler to see in political activity a means for solving his problems. This process of increasing political awareness and activity has accelerated remarkably in the Northeast during the last ten years, and has penetrated most deeply in rural areas close to large urban centers, such as the Mata and the Agreste.

The convergence of the two factors indicated—the social irrationality of agricultural development, and the growing political awakening of the rural masses—is responsible for the formation of a revolutionary potential in the Northeast during the last few years. The evolution of this potential will depend on the historical conditions prevailing, not only in the Northeast, but in the country as a whole. Nevertheless, there is no indication that the ruling groups are psychologically equipped to launch solutions that are far-reaching enough to alter the course of the principal forces. The accumulation of these forces will continue inexorably and their mere existence will weigh increasingly on the political process. Once a certain irreversible point has been reached, history can no longer fulfill itself through the conventional methods, and an era of unforeseeable happenings will be initiated, in which the speed of events will reduce to almost nil the effectiveness of any rational leadership.

Notes

INTRODUCTION

[1] After the military coup of April, 1964, new laws were enacted which were aimed at eliminating the small political parties and introducing the principle of absolute majority for the election of the President of the Republic.

CHAPTER 1 (pp. 3–12)

[1] Jean-Paul Sartre, *Critique de la Raison Dialectique* (Paris: Gallimard, 1960), p. 373. In the same sense Lukacs states that "practice constitutes the criterion of theoretical truth: the exactitude or inexactitude of the reflex in thinking on objective reality that exists independently of our conscious minds, or better still, our closeness to the truth can be measured only in and through practice." *La Destruction de la Raison* (Paris: L'Arche Editeur, 1958), vol. 1, p. 23.

[2] Georges Lukacs, *Histoire et Conscience de Classe.* Cited by Jean-Paul Sartre in *Marxisme et Existencialisme* (Paris: Plon, 1962), p. 3.

[3] Jean-Paul Sartre, *Marxisme et Existencialisme,* p. 6.

[4] See especially Marx's Preface to *Contribution to the Critique of Political Economy* (1859), French trans. Laura Lafargue (Paris: Marcel Giard, 1928).

[5] Bronislaw Malinowsky, "Culture" in *Encyclopedia of the Social Sciences* (New York: Macmillan, 1936).

[6] W. F. Ogburn, "Social Change" in *Encyclopedia of the Social Sciences* (New York: Macmillan, 1936).

[7] See the letter to Joseph Bloch dated September 21, 1890, in *Etudes Philosophiques* (Paris: Editions sociales, 1947), p. 123.

[8] Melville J. Herskovits, "The Processes of Cultural Change" in *The Science of Man in the World Crises,* ed. Ralph Linton (New York: Columbia University Press, 1945), pp. 164–167.

[9] Everett F. Hagen, *On the Theory of Social Change* (Illinois: Dorsey Press, 1962), p. 505.

[10] Gunnar Myrdal, "An American Dilemma," Appendix 3, pp. 1065–1070, edited in *Value in Social Theory* (London: Routledge and Kegan Paul, 1958), pp. 198–205.

[11] *Ibid.,* p. 204.

[12] *Critique of Political Economy,* p. 334.

CHAPTER 3 (pp. 22–38)

[1] "Ludwig Feuerbach and the Outcome of Classical German Philosophy," in *Etudes Philosophiques* (Paris: Editions sociales, 1947), p. 47.

[2] This point was very properly suggested by Stanislaw Ossowski, professor of sociology at the University of Warsaw, in a recent book: "It is easy to overlook the fact that the concept of the class struggle, the basic concept for Marxian doctrine, comprises two different categories of historical process. The first includes liberation struggles within the framework of the perennial conflict between the oppressing classes and the oppressed classes; the second includes struggles between classes competing for power in a society with a multi-divisional structure." *Class Structure in the Social Consciousness* (London: Routledge and Kegan Paul, 1963), p. 84.

[3] Friedrich Engels, *The Origin of the Family, Private Property and the State,* French trans. A. M. Desrousseaux (Paris: Alfred Costes, 1946), p. 223.

[4] *Ibid.,* p. 227.

[5] *Ibid.*

[6] Max Weber, *Economia y Sociedad,* Spanish trans. José Ferrater Mora (Mexico: Fondo de Cultura Económica, 1944), vol. IV, p. 116.

[7] S. M. Lipset, *Political Man* (London: Mercury Books, 1963), p. 21.

[8] N. Lenin, *The State and Revolution* (Moscow: Foreign Language Editions, 1947) in *Selected Works,* French ed., vol. II, p. 201.

[9] Karl Mannheim, *Freedom, Power and Democratic Planning,* Spanish trans. Manuel Durán Gil (Mexico: Fondo de Cultura Económica, 1953), p. 109.

[10] N. Lenin, *What Is to be Done?* in *Selected Works* (Moscow: Foreign Language Editions, 1947), vol. I, p. 284.

CHAPTER 4 (pp. 39–46)

[1] Karl Marx, *Etudes Philosophiques* (Paris: Editions sociales, 1947), p. 57.

[2] See the 1895 Introduction to Marx's *Class Struggles in France, 1848–1850,* French trans. (Paris: Editions sociales, 1946), p. 12.

[3] Friedrich Engels, *Revolution and Counter-Revolution in Germany,* French trans. J. Molitor (Paris: Alfred Costes, 1933), p. 10.

[4] Introduction to *Class Struggles,* pp. 11–12.

[5] *Ibid.*

[6] Marx, Preface to *Contribution to the Critique of Political Economy* (1859), French trans. Laura Lafargue (Paris: Marcel Giard, 1928).

[7] *Ibid.*

[8] *Revolution and Counter-Revolution,* pp. 19–20.

[9] N. Lenin, *What Is to be Done?* in *Selected Works* (Moscow: Foreign Language Editions, 1947), vol. I, p. 217.

[10] *Ibid.,* pp. 205–206.

[11] *Ibid.,* p. 207.

[12] *Ibid.,* p. 278. Although Marx and Engels considered the revolutions of the past to be the work of minority groups, at no point did they consider the technique of the "coup de main," as a method that could be used by the workers to ascend to power. Engels' criticism of the "Blanquists," holding them partly responsible for the failure of the 1871 Commune, is well known: "Educated in the school of conspiracy," he writes, "linked by the discipline needed for so many things, they operated on the principle that a relatively small group of men, well organized and able, would be in a position, not only to take over the helm of State at short notice, but also by vigorous application and overrunning everything to maintain themselves in power for a sufficient period to succeed in enlisting the masses on the side of the Revolution and ranging it behind the small ruling group." Introduction (1891) to Marx's 1871 *Civil War in France,* French trans. (Paris: Editions sociales, 1946) p. 17.

After the Second Congress of the Russian Social Democrats in 1903, when the division was made between Bolsheviks and Menchevites, and from the time of the publication of *What Is to be Done?* in the previous year, Lenin began to be accused of Jacobinism and Blanquism. He considered the first accusation a compliment but always defended himself against the second, even as late as 1917, when he wrote his famous article, "On the Duality of Power." It would be wrong to classify the Bolshevik take-over of power in

October as a Blanquist coup, since the revolutionary fervor of the people was so great that Kerensky's government fell like a dead leaf. We could designate as "Blanquist" the action of Lenin's group during the whole revolutionary period, from the fall of Czarism when, through the activities of a small minority, he managed in four or five months to control the Soviets of the big cities by taking advantage of the discredit of a government that, with the continuation of the war, was daily losing its legitimacy and never achieved any degree of effectiveness. Lenin's specific action was not in capturing power (which in any case would have changed hands at that time) but keeping himself in power, which can only be accounted for if we bear in mind his extraordinary qualities of leadership, the power that the socialist doctrine demonstrated as an instrument to unify the action of the masses, and the challenge offered by foreign invasion of Russian soil during the Civil War.

[13] When he said good-bye to a group of Swiss students in 1917, before his departure for a Russia already in the throes of the revolutionary process, Lenin said that his generation would not live to see the establishment of socialism. See citation in Isaac Deutsch's *Stalin* (New York: Vintage Books, 1960).

[14] *On the Duality of Power and Letters on Tactics* in *Complete Works,* English trans. (Moscow: Lenin Institute), vol. XX, Bk. I, p. 121.

[15] *Ibid.,* vol. XXXI, Bk. I, p. 68.

[16] *Revolution and Counter-Revolution,* p. 11.

CHAPTER 6 (pp. 63–73)

[1] Friedrich Engels, *Revolution and Counter-Revolution in Germany,* French trans. J. Molitor (Paris: Alfred Costes, 1933), p. 15.

[2] N. Lenin, *What Is to be Done?* in *Selected Works,* vol. I, p. 275.

[3] *Ibid.,* p. 263.

[4] Francisco Julião, an extremely influential Peasant League leader from 1962 (translator's note).

CHAPTER 7 (pp. 77–95)

[1] The figures used for indicating income per capita and conversion rates are based on statistics compiled by the United Nations Economic Committee for Latin America. See *El Desarollo Económico de América Latina en la Postguerra,* vol. II, May, 1963.

[2] For the basic figures, see P. N. Rosenstein-Rodan, "International Aid for Underdeveloped Countries," in *Review of Economics and Statistics,* May, 1961.

[3] *El Desarollo Económico,* vol. I, tables 64 and 65.

[4] *Loc. cit.*

[5] One hectare is equal to 2.471 acres (translator's note).

[6] See *Los Recursos Naturales en América Latina, su Conocimiento Actual y Investigaciones Necesarias en este Campo,* ECLA, vol. II, 1963.

[7] *Ibid.*

[8] *Ibid.*, vol. I.

CHAPTER 8 (pp. 96–124)

[1] Joaquim Murtinho, Minister of Finance in the Campos Sales government (1898–1902) succeeded in reestablishing the government's credit abroad after ten years of acute inflation.

[2] A privileged exchange rate *theoretically* based on the true cost of acquiring exchange through exports (translator's note).

CHAPTER 9 (pp. 125–162)

[1] Literally, "dwellers," the implication being that the resident merely occupies the land, but has no rights. The words "tenant" and "settlers" contain some of the same connotations (translator's note).

[2] Literally, men who live under a condition (translator's note).

[3] Regions of the Northeast. A full description of these regions is given in the second and third sections of this chapter (translator's note).

[4] Extending social legislation to apply to rural workers (translator's note).

[5] At the end of 1964 there was a substantial drop in international sugar prices. The "sugar barons" of the Northeast took advantage of the country's altered political situation to evade the provisions of the minimum wage law, thus taking from the workers the social conquests they had recently achieved. As a result, a situation of social tension was created far more serious than that which had led to the the formation of the Peasant Leagues during the second half of the 'fifties (C. F., May, 1965).

[6] Mata, literally "woodland" (translator's note).

[7] Caatinga—a kind of scrub forest consisting of drought-

resisting vegetation of thorny shrubs and dwarf trees. In more moist areas it forms dense, and sometimes impenetrable, thickets. In the more arid localities the twisted trees disappear altogether and cacti predominate. As the dry season sets in, the grasses wither, the trees lose their leaves, and by the end of the season the caatinga has a bare, desolate look (translator's note).

[8] Agreste, literally "wild region." It is covered by a sub-xerophytic vegetation in the form of woodland, bearing tall trees, with a vigorous undergrowth (translator's note).

[9] The Sertão is the dry interior. The term has no specific meaning and is not easy to define. For practical purposes it can be taken to describe the backlands, that is, the dry hilly uplands above the Caatinga, with their natural vegetation of brushwood and grasses, interspersed with belts and patches of caatinga. However, no description of the things physically present in the Sertão can give the full meaning of the word. It is also a state of mind, and the "Sertanejo" (the dweller in the Sertão) has figured prominently in the literature and folklore of Brazil.

[10] Serras, literally "mountains," are mountain ridges which because of their elevation, receive a more regular and abundant rainfall. They are therefore reasonably well watered and may be likened to oases in the Sertão (translator's note).

[11] The "winter" is the rainy season (translator's note).

[12] As early as 1909, the Federal Inspectorate of Drought Protection Works was set up to undertake studies of the problems of the Northeast (translator's note).

[13] The local political and economic boss (translator's note).

[14] Municipalities are legally entitled to a proportion of federal income tax (translator's note).